Hi Kent!

welcome!

[signature]

THANKS FOR LISTENING!

Thanks for Listening!

Jack Brickhouse
with Jack Rosenberg and Ned Colletti

DIAMOND COMMUNICATIONS, INC.
SOUTH BEND, INDIANA

1986

THANKS FOR LISTENING!

Manufactured in the United States of America

Diamond Communications, Inc.
Post Office Box 88
South Bend, Indiana 46624
(219) 287-5008

Library of Congress Cataloging-in-Publication Data

Brickhouse, Jack, 1916–
    Thanks for listening!

    1. Brickhouse, Jack, 1916–   . 2. Sportscasters –
United States – Biography.   I. Rosenberg, Jack, 1926–
II. Colletti, Ned.   III. Title.
GV742.42.B75A37   1986   070.4′49796′0924 [B]   86-2103
ISBN 0-912083-16-6

To Daisy.
God couldn't be everywhere so he created Mothers.

Jack Brickhouse
Mini-Chronology

Year	Station	Feature
1937-40	WMBD, Peoria	Bradley basketball and Illinois prep sports
1940-43	WGN Radio	Cubs and White Sox
1942-43 46-47	WGN Radio	Big 10 football
1945	WJJD Radio	White Sox Notre Dame football
1946	WMCA Radio, NY	New York Giants baseball
1947	WBKB-TV	Cubs
1948-56	WGN-TV & DuMont Network	Pro Wrestling
1948-67	WGN-TV	White Sox
1948-81	WGN-TV	Cubs
1953-76	WGN Radio	Bears

Contents

Publisher's Note

I am not the publisher of this book. But my wife, Jill, is President of Diamond Communications and she said I could pinch-hit for her on this one. She knows that being a Cub fan has been a way of life for me since I was eleven. And she knows that my pantheon of heroes enshrines Bert Wilson, Jack Quinlan, Vince and Lou, and, at the center, Jack Brickhouse.

As he did for millions of fans, Jack taught me, over the airwaves, how to keep the game in perspective and how to enjoy it, win or lose. The Cubs helped Jack illustrate how to side with the underdog and that doing so is not the same as being satisfied with mediocrity.

In 1980, my appreciative history of the Cubs, *The Game Is Never Over*, was published. I was worried that, as a complete unknown fan and certainly not a member of the Chicago sports media, my book would be met with silence or perhaps even mild hostility. After all, any one of the old pros in Chicago could have written a history of the Cubs, left-handed.

The publisher sent a copy of the galley proofs to Jack Brickhouse, who was on the road in Atlanta. What did Jack do? He called the publisher and said he loved the book and would be glad to have me join him in the booth during the next homestand. I couldn't believe it.

Maybe it sounds a little too "Gee Whiz," but that was one of the great days in my life.

As I went through the press gate at Wrigley Field, I saw Jack and introduced myself to him. He put his hand on my shoulder and introduced me around as one of the greatest Cub fans in the world. This from a man who has forgotten more than I'll ever know about the Cubs. And his kindness didn't stop there. He made me feel at home in the booth, let me talk about the book on the air and then gave it a resounding plug. That is Jack Brickhouse—a kind, warm human being, always with an encouraging word for a rookie.

Another person in the booth that day was WGN's crack sports editor, Jack Rosenberg. His distinguished career has always been behind the scenes making certain that the job got done right. He has been the quarterback on this book project and in the process gained the gratitude and friendship of everyone at Diamond.

Even though he wasn't in the booth that day, we are grateful to Ned Colletti for his involvement. As a life-long Cub fan, Ned knows what talent it took to breathe life into some of the Cub teams of the past.

Jack has that talent: always has, always will. As you'll discover in this book, he is really a man for all seasons.

Jim Langford

"If we had to earn the privilege of speech by the weight of our words, I wonder how many of us would be mute?"

Gomer Bath, WMBD, Peoria, Illinois.

Foreword

Retirement was upon me. It was winter, 1981. The shadows had lengthened. They inevitably do in a man's lifetime. Much like the shadows that engulf the void between the mound and home plate at Wrigley Field on a late summer afternoon.

I was hearing the last hurrahs. Testimonials. A hundred or more. It almost got to be a joke. An emcee would stand and say something like: "Tonight we honor Jack Brickhouse—again and again."

I loved every nostalgic moment, every plaque, every scroll, every piece of luggage.

But can a man who has been extremely active ever fully prepare for retirement?

I had pondered that question.

Gardening was out. My only acquaintance with tomatoes and green peppers had been at the dinner table. Besides, let's see you plant crops on Lake Shore Drive.

There was golf, but I knew golf wasn't the same when you played every day without having to sneak out of the office to get to the first tee.

There was travel, but somehow even that wouldn't be the same when you didn't have to worry about when to return.

And how many times can you read literature from Social Security or AARP (American Association of Retired Persons)?

Do you get the picture?

Then came the rescue. There was this testimonial for me at the Chicago Press Club. A Who's Who of the media world was there, maybe 300 or more. The keynote speaker was Stanton Cook, president of the Tribune Company, parent company of WGN. I won't ever forget that night.

Stan Cook gave me a memorable sendoff. He said that I had been the eternal optimist. He said that I had worn rose-colored glasses through the years in my coverage of the Cubs. He said my loyalty was such that in my mind the Cubs had won every game every season.

At the tail end of his remarks, he paused, looked at me and said: "We can't retire Jack Brickhouse because you can't retire a legend!"

That brought the crowd to its feet, stomping and whistling. Tears streamed down my face. I was overwhelmed.

The applause lasted for what seemed to me an eternity. Then Stan added: "You know, Jack, it's obvious from this tremendous reception you've gotten here tonight that we can't let you retire. So why not take a month's vacation and then let's you and I get together with Jim Dowdle, the president of Tribune Broadcasting, and see what we can work out to keep you active at WGN."

I almost passed out. I had escaped retirement! And the company wound up paying me a bigger salary than I had received in my broadcasting heyday. Or hey-hey day, if you will.

My career took a turn in the road from that point on. No more play-by-play but a variety of special assignment features for radio and television, a multitude of speaking engagements and heavy involvement with various Cubs' projects, including the Cubs' Die-Hard Fan Club and its tens of thousands of loyal members.

For me, there always will be a certain trauma connected with being away from the day-to-day grind of the sports beat. When the Cubs clinched the NL East at Pittsburgh in September of '84, I longed to be at the mike hollering: "On your feet, everybody, this is it. Rick Sutcliffe, bless him, has done it again. I'll be back with the happy totals . . ."

I am most appreciative of the fact that long-time friends like Harry Caray and Vince Lloyd and Lou Boudreau and Steve Stone and DeWayne Staats and, before he moved on to Houston, Milo Hamilton have shown me extreme kindness on my visits to the broadcast booths rather than treating me like a ship that has passed in the night. The Cubs dedicated the television booth to me in '82, and there's a plaque on the door to that effect, but I understand that entitles me only to so many privileges. I have resigned myself to the reality that no more will I face that camera on the ramp and wait for a cue.

When I walked down the ramp after my final baseball telecast in 1981, I was besieged for autographs by young and old alike. It was exhilarating and it was sad. Television crews from all the Chicago stations followed my every step. They knew the grand old man had just called his final inning.

I went directly to the Pink Poodle, where the media hangs out at Wrigley Field, but then I was summoned by a thousand fans or more to stick my head out of the Poodle and take one more bow. What a feeling. Tantamount, I guess, to a ball player being called from the dugout to acknowledge the crowd after he has hit a home run.

Back in my office later, I reread a letter I had received from a Cubs' fan in Hinsdale. His words struck home:

Dear Mr. Brickhouse,

Since hearing of your imminent retirement I have wanted to write this letter to say thanks for everything. I have put off writing until now, I think, in the hope that I was somehow imagining your leaving Cubs' baseball—that somehow I would awaken and the realization of your leaving would be gone. Sad to say I have come to the realization that in two weeks you will be gone.

I have been a Cub fan for most of my 30 years. My earliest memories of home involve my watching the game with my mother while she ironed or went about her other household chores. Ernie Banks was our favorite player in those days, so we always took particular delight whenever you would Hey-Hey one of his home runs.

I was with you when Don Cardwell pitched his no-hitter in his first day as a Cub. I was with you when Banks hit his 400th and 500th home runs. I was with you when the home umpire blew a strike call and Milt Pappas' perfect game. I was with you when Don Young lost that fly ball in the sun in 1969.

Like any lifelong friend, you were with me in good times and in bad. Whenever life was a mystery to me you would bring me joy and reason with a story about Hack Wilson or Tinker or Evers or Chance. While you don't know me personally, we've been through a lot together, you and me. You have been a trusted mentor and friend.

Saying a final goodbye to a friend is one of life's most difficult and deflating experiences. But it has to be done. Again, thanks for everything, Mr. Brickhouse. Goodbye and God-speed.

Sincerely,

Jack Wallin

The only thing I can say to the Jack Wallins of this world is "Thanks for Listening. . . ."

Jack Brickhouse

I
Playing in Peoria

I'm sorry I wasn't born in a log cabin. I could
have gotten a lot of mileage out of it. Instead, my
first public appearance came at Methodist Hospital
in Peoria, Illinois. That's where I was born. The
date was January 24, 1916. I came into the world
as John Beasley Brickhouse. I was named after my
father, John William (Will) Brickhouse, and my
grandfather, Beasley Brickhouse. Years later, I
would be told by a radio station executive to drop
the name of Brickhouse for broadcasting purposes.
He said it wouldn't catch on. I'm glad I didn't heed
his advice. Somehow, even today, I can't imagine
being introduced as John Beasley.

Grandpa Beasley, I understand, held the
mythical state record for prominent failures in
the state of Tennessee. He was a director of a
now non-existent museum, pastor of a now non-
existent church and president of a now non-
existent college. To top it off, he fought and was
wounded on the Confederate side in the Civil
War.

The Brickhouses resided in Clarksville, Tennessee, and my father, Will, ran away from home
repeatedly, lured by an itch for show business. He

left permanently at the age of 14. One of his uncles once found him working with a hypnotist in the window of a department store. The hypnotist would use his alleged supernatural powers to overcome gravity with feats of levitation. Will Brickhouse was the subject, the illusory object floating in the air as the small-town crowds gaped in wonderment.

My father ran the gamut of the entertainment world. He was a sideshow barker. He was buried alive. He was a carnival man's carnival man. He ran concessions at White City when that great amusement park was in its hey-day in Chicago's early days. He originated "split week vaudeville." In that era, the acts on a vaudeville bill would contract for a minimum of one week. But in smaller communities, most folks had seen the show by Thursday or Friday, so the bill would die the rest of the week. Out of economic necessity, Will Brickhouse got the idea of splitting up the week by bringing in a fresh show mid-week. This turned out to be the savior of the small house. And without the small house, which was the only training ground, there could have been no big house.

Here and there I still hear an old-time gagster wisecrack: "I can get you a split week in Mattoon. You follow Fink's Mules."

I find it fascinating to leaf through my father's clippings and ads and letters and contracts. He dealt with the big names of his day. Occasionally, a grizzled veteran would stop me and ask: "With a name like yours, could you have been related to Will Brickhouse?" And when I filled him in, he would say: "Let me tell you about your father."

Invariably, it was a story of some escapade that required police intervention before terminating. A man who later became president of a Hollywood movie studio told me that he and Will Brickhouse took over the job of directing traffic at State and Madison in Chicago the night of the World War I armistice. They finally were arrested.

My mother, Daisy, was an immigrant from Cardiff, Wales. Her father, like many Welshmen, had followed the coal mines to America. Daisy and her mother joined him here later. My maternal grandfather was killed in the Cherry Mines disaster at Cherry, Illinois, one of the great catastrophies in mining history.

Daisy got a job behind a cigar counter at a travelling man's hotel in Peoria. She was 15 then. She stood 5-1, weighed some 90 pounds. Will Brickhouse was 39 then. He stood 6-5, weighed some 225 pounds. He was a travelling man and stayed at the hotel where Daisy worked. They met once, he left town, then he returned three weeks later and married her. The marriage didn't have a chance of lasting.

Not only were their ages and physical dimensions totally different, so, too, were their philosophies of life. Will Brickhouse was an outgoing type, a super salesman who won and lost shows and acts in card games or crap games, a man who enjoyed the company of the hail-fellow-well-met variety. He simply didn't take care of himself. He died of pneumonia in Chicago at the age of 42. I was only two. My parents were separated at the time of his death.

I regret to this day that my father died before

I was old enough to really know him. I am convinced, from what I've learned about him over the years, that his creativity and salesmanship would have made him a natural for the entertainment world as we know it today. John Balaban of the famous Balaban & Katz theatre chain told me some years ago that Will Brickhouse taught him the rudiments of selling film. "I learned more from your dad than anyone else," said John. "He took me under his wing. I never was treated better." John Balaban and I became great friends when he learned I was Will's son. In fact, my first television appearances were on his station, WBKB, inasmuch as it was the only Chicago station at that time.

As for Daisy Brickhouse, she was brave and proud. Here she was, a widowed teenager with a small son. It was a tough deal. Daisy earned $14 per week as a food checker, cashier and hostess at the hotel. Her job as a checker was to guard the company's interest against all sorts of connivers. Even the would-be cheaters respected her dedication and honesty. She was a gem.

Grandma lived with us and she served as a cook at Proctor Hospital in Peoria. I spent lots of days after school delivering food trays to the patients. It was a good way to keep from getting hungry.

The fact that Daisy remarried solved very little, inasmuch as destiny frowned on her once again and the marriage eventually was dissolved.

I still love to quote Daisy's line when a friend congratulated her on raising me even though times were tough. She said: "It's a poor hen that can't scratch for one chick."

Daisy placed high emphasis on my educational pursuits and fortunately Peoria enjoyed a solid school system. I knew better than to bring home poor grades. And even with all the economic ups and downs, my childhood was pleasant. Admittedly, I was somewhat of a schemer, and the inheriting of my father's sales pitch showed up early.

It was 1927. Charles Lindbergh had just made the first non-stop solo flight across the Atlantic, New York to Paris. The *Peoria Journal* recruited every kid it could find to sell extra papers. I was 11 then, and very impressionable, and when the extras sold like hotcakes, I figured the newspaper business was for me. After all, I had bought the papers for two cents and sold them for three, plus tips. What a way to make a fast buck. I took a paper route. One problem: it was in a residential area, so I was limited. A fixed income didn't appeal to me. I gave up the regular route after a week and headed for the downtown office buildings. Even at 11, I had discovered that's where the action was.

I ran into a roadblock almost immediately. There already were other newsboys in the lobbies of those office buildings and they were older and bigger. I went up and down the corridors anyhow and sold my share until this big guy stopped me and warned: "If you come back here tomorrow night and try to sell papers, I'm going to kick you right in the butt." He was as good as his word. I came back the next night and he kicked me in the butt. I ran two blocks to the police station and luckily encountered a husky Irish cop who listened intently to my sob story. Tears were streaming down my face. It was an Academy Award performance. The officer was deeply sympathetic. He returned to the office building with me, held this startled competitor of mine at arm's length and growled: "If you ever so much as harm a hair on this kid's head again, I'll throw you in jail and lose the key." I had a free hand after that and the Jefferson Building, in particular, provided daily money-making opportunities.

I owned one other distinction: I was probably the neatest-dressed newsboy in town. My mother insisted that cleanliness was next to Godliness. Believe it or not, she made me wear a clean shirt with a necktie to peddle papers. That made an impression on many of my customers. My weekly take rose to five dollars, based on selling 75 to 100 papers nightly, five nights a week. Big money in those days.

I sold both the *Peoria Journal* and *Peoria Star*. I would get my papers at the Journal Building. The men behind the counters were Charlie Caley for the *Journal* and Big Heinie for the *Star*. Caley later owned WMBD in Peoria, my first broadcasting home. He would ask: "How many papers can you take tonight?" If I would ask for 35, he would say: "Can't you take 45?" Big Heinie would do the same thing with the *Star*. You could return unsold papers but they frowned on it and I normally stuck around until my whole bag was gone.

The major newspaper distributorship in Peoria was owned by the Hartman brothers. They controlled most of the newsstands at choice locations. Word of my enterprising tactics had reached the Hartmans and they offered me a job at more money. I had learned the Hartman boys had bought a $25,000 home for their mother. "Is that story true?" I asked Mr. Hartman. He nodded in the affirmative. "Well," I said, "I hope to build a $25,000 home for my mother some day and I figure the best way to do it is to be in business for myself, just like you." Mr. Hartman patted me on the shoulder and laughed. "Kid," he said, "I think maybe this town is big enough for both of us. I think you're going to make it, all right."

There were other signs, too, that I had inherited my father's enterprising spirit and my mother's determination. For example, I remember the time our sixth grade class at Lincoln Grammar School decided to sell pencils in order to buy a volleyball for the girls and a basketball for the boys. A pencil set was offered as first prize to the student selling the most pencils. I broke my wrist that same week while trying to hop a ride on a newspaper truck. The cast on my arm turned out to be a bonanza. I stuck pencils underneath the cast and visited my newspaper customers with a sad look on my face. I played it to the hilt. Instead of getting a nickel for a pencil, I frequently got a dime or even a quarter. I won the pencil set and made what to me was a small fortune besides. They almost had to rip that cast off me. I would have worn it for a year.

I finally quit the newspaper business to become a caddy at the urging of my chum, Stanley Cox. When I went to the *Journal* circulation department to inform them this would be my last night as a carrier, Big Heinie, who doled out the papers, said: "How about taking another kid around to show him where to sell? You know, break him in on the job." I answered: "Why should I? Let him work up the route the same way I did." I turned around to walk away and Big Heinie kicked me in the butt. So my newspaper career started and ended with a kick in the butt!

My big love in sports was basketball. All I ever wanted under the tree at Christmas was a new basketball. We used to play outdoors on the cement courts at Lincoln Grammar School and it was the old story: if you had a ball, you were guaranteed to play. I had a lot of Jewish friends. They would go to Hebrew School on Saturday morning at Agudas Achim Synagogue, then come over to Lincoln for basketball in the afternoon. It's funny what a man recollects from his childhood days, but I still recall an incident in which one of the bigger boys slapped me for missing a sleeper shot that would have won the pick-up game. Benny Schwartz, later a legendary athletic hero on Peoria Manual Training High School's state championship basketball team, decked my assailant with a right to the jaw and told him to pick on someone his own size.

Peoria in those days was known as the "Red Light Capital" of the Midwest. I lived two blocks away from a district populated almost entirely by ladies of the evening. When you walked down the street, they would rap on the windows with rings to attract your attention. Even the little kids knew there was something different about these houses. As a sophomore at Peoria Manual, I used to wait for a streetcar on a corner in the red light district. There was this one heavy-set madam who invariably sat on her porch at 7:45 in the morning for what I assume was a well-earned rest. She would pleasantly say "good morning" as I stood on the corner and that went on for several days until one time she asked: "How's school?" I answered: "Just fair. I'm having trouble with geometry." Said the madam: "Let me see the assignment you have for today." Cautiously, I walked up onto her porch, showed her a couple of tough problems—and she figured them out in a matter of seconds. It turned out that she was a math shark. I can now confess that the madam helped me pass geometry at Manual. She really knew how to work out those geometric propositions, if you'll pardon the expression.

I was captivated by speech and dramatics in high school. I had the lead in the class play, a Lionel Barrymore-type part of an elderly man, because I was one of the few whose voice had changed. I know now that a course in public speaking should be mandatory at the high school level. It teaches you how to stand on your feet and address a group. It is amazing how many can't do it.

High school speech courses taught me the basic importance of learning your audience and your surroundings. I lost out in the National Forensic League state prep championships at Northwestern as a result of trying to use the same voice projection in front of a small group of judges that I had used in rehearsing in a 500-seat auditorium. I talked right through and over the judges and that did me in. But I learned a good lesson.

What a debt of gratitude I owe Hazel Conrad, the speech teacher, and Lily Dean, the dramatics teacher, and Gertrude Applegate, the English teacher. They changed my life at Manual. I recall that Miss Applegate called me in one day during my senior year and said: "I've been following your career at Manual and I'm convinced your future lies in the entertainment world. I would like to see you go to a New York dramatics school. I don't have much money myself, but if you can raise half the tuition, I will be glad to provide the other half."

I turned down the offer—at that point in time I wanted to become the world's greatest lawyer—but over the years I have come to realize what a magnificent gesture this was on the part of a teacher who could ill-afford it financially.

I captained the swimming team at Manual and we were just good enough to avoid drowning. I vividly recall a dual meet against our arch rival, Peoria Central, at the Peoria YMCA pool. They had the state backstroke champion, Frank Blust. He and I were the lone entrants at 100 yards and the only reason I agreed was that first place was worth five points and second place three points—so all I had to do to get the three points was finish the five lengths. Frank passed me three times and was out of the shower and talking to his girlfriend before I negotiated the distance. But I got a big ovation for accepting public humiliation for the sake of three points!

I was graduated from Manual in 1933 in tough times. I decided to enter Bradley Tech, now Bradley University, only after Bradley's president, Dr. Frederick Hamilton, promised me a job. Daisy signed a note at a loan company to get the funds for my matriculation fee and books. A wonderful Peorian by the name of Milo Reeve, who had helped many youngsters, co-signed my note at Bradley to guarantee the tuition.

The job promise fell through. Every time I tried to talk to Dr. Hamilton, he was unavailable or too busy. I never did get to see him again. Meanwhile, the Bradley business office kept calling me for the tuition money, which at that time was $100 per semester. It might as well have been a million. I finally obtained a dishwashing job at the Pere Marquette Hotel, where Daisy worked. I washed dishes from 5 A.M. until noon, attended classes from 1 P.M. to 7 P.M., and managed to work out some with the Bradley freshman basketball team in an effort to work my way into an athletic scholarship. Then I would study until midnight and get up at 4:30 to do it all over again.

I lost 20 pounds off an already skinny frame. The grind was too much. I couldn't hack it. I left Bradley after one semester. I became a soda jerk. That didn't last. I broke too many glasses and got into a fist fight with a customer who said I was clumsy. I went to Hiram Walker's Distillery to fill bottles with gin. It worked on a siphon principle. Before long, I was sucking on the nozzle so the gin would flow. I got a snootful. They had to call a doctor. Since that episode, I've laid off gin. It is ironic that a few years back, I spoke at a testimonial for Jack Musick, the retired president of Hiram Walker's. He stood at the podium and took credit for my broadcasting career. "If we wouldn't have fired this bum years ago," laughed Musick, "he'd still be working at Hiram Walker's!"

Following my fling at Hiram Walker's, I signed up for the CCC, the Civilian Conservation Corps. That failed to pan out, either. Then came what developed into my major break. Radio station WMBD in Peoria staged a "So You Want To Be An Announcer" contest. I entered, figured that if I could win the $50 first prize wristwatch, I might hock it for $30 and get enough of a stake to go to the West Coast.

WMBD held six preliminary contests, six contestants in each. I won a preliminary. That left six finalists and four prizes. Harold (Fuzz) Livingston, a National Forensic League champion with whom I had caddied, won the announcing contest going away. I finished fifth. I know why. I fell on my face in the part where you had to ad lib for two minutes about some kind of jewelry tool. I couldn't even identify it, let alone talk about it. I found out then and there that it's important to be able to ad lib. Since then ad lib has helped earn me a living.

The aftermath of that contest is that the folks

at WMBD heard something in my delivery which prompted them to invite me to work at the station on a one week trial basis without pay. That led to a second week without pay. When they asked me to work a third week, I balked. I needed employment and money. I told them I had an opportunity to return to the Pere Marquette as a busboy. If they had let me go, I suppose the entire course of my life would have been altered. WMBD decided to pay me $17 per week as a part-time announcer, part-time switchboard operator. I jumped at the chance. I received that paycheck, changed it into 170 dimes, then visited my favorite pool hall, bent on fulfilling a longtime ambition to hit the jackpot on the dime slot machine. I came up with the cherries a couple of times and the oranges once and that was it. My $17 disappeared. Next week I did the same thing. Now my $34 had been swallowed by the mechanical bandit. That cured me before the slots could become a bad habit.

By 1938, I was well-established in Peoria broadcasting. I was the only sports announcer at the only station in town. I was single and had life by the tail on a downhill pull. My weekly salary was $46. My wonderful grandmother was gone but Daisy and I were getting along fine. I decided to buy a used car. I financed it through Lincoln Loan Company at $20.01 per month. The girl in charge at this loan office was a real beauty named Nelda Teach. I had trouble making the car payments but it was a pleasure to visit Lincoln Loan and explain my financial predicaments because it gave me an excuse to see Nelda. I had met her once before on a blind double date but she was with the other guy. The car ultimately was repossessed, but the car be damned, I was in love. Nelda and I were married in 1939. We borrowed a car and eloped to Bessemer, Michigan. I also borrowed the money from Nelda to pay for the license and the fee for the probate judge whom we awakened from his afternoon nap to marry us.

Our marriage was blessed with one daughter, Jeanne. She has the education I always wanted. In retrospect, I can say that Nelda was a loving wife and mother—and a great lady. But the chemistry wasn't there in the latter years of our lengthy marriage. The fact that my job kept me on the road so much no doubt played a significant role in the break-up, even though I hesitate to say that lest it be construed as a copout. In any case, I later married Pat Ettelson, who ran her own public relations firm. She is fun-loving and outgoing and has been not only my wife but my close friend as well. It has been a marriage that really works. She knows more about sports than I do. As for Daisy, she passed away in 1973. God, how I miss her!

Actually, I began dictating my memoirs in 1976, the year of the Bicentennial. Maybe I chose that year because there are those who insist I have been on the air at least 200 years. I will make this point: if I had to spend 200 years in one job, I would pray it be as a sports announcer. And at WGN! But that is getting ahead of the story. Of my earlier career, let me say this: you haven't lived until you've frozen your posterior off conducting Lowenstein Furniture's "Man on the Street" program on icy winter days in Peoria.

Gomer Bath had originated the show on WMBD, admitting he got the idea from the *Chicago Tribune*'s Inquiring Reporter column. When Gomer moved to higher responsibilities at the station, I became the "Man on the Street." Every broadcast was an adventure.

It was a 15-minute feature and in bleak weather I was lucky if a stray dog wandered past my perch on South Adams Street. I compensated in these situations by hauling Lowenstein's salesmen out of the store to keep me company on the air. They would assume phony names, phony occupations and phony ethnic backgrounds and shoot the breeze about the trials and tribulations of the world.

The standing joke around the store was that proprietor Jack Lowenstein refused to hire a salesman unless he could do at least three dialects!

In looking back, I realize that "Man on the Street" gave me a better indoctrination into the art of ad libbing than any assignment in my career. It was live, all live, and I had to expect the unexpected.

There was the time I interviewed an elderly lady who was the Grandmother-of-the-Year type. White hair, specs, shawl, the whole bit. I asked: "What is your favorite recipe for Christmas cookies?" She snapped back: "Never mind that. When in the hell are you people going to do something about the damned hoodlums in this town?"

And I can't forget the inevitable farmer who happened by in the midst of a long summer dry spell. My question: "How do you explain this terrible drought we have around here right now?" And his answer: "No rain."

The show helped rid me of an amateurish interviewing habit. I discovered I was repeating, unnecessarily, what a guest had said in order to stall long enough to think of my next question. Example:

Brickhouse: "What do you do for a living?"

Answer: "Well, I'm a plumber and I'm going to fix a toilet."

Brickhouse: "Oh, so you're a plumber and you're going to fix a toilet."

I'm lucky I quit this habit before one of my radio guests just walked away shaking his head.

I stayed with "Man on the Street" almost five years, the last couple in conjunction with Howard Dorsey. WMBD added Howard to help bail me out. We interviewed each other frequently, imitated people from all walks and made the most of a limited storehouse of jokes. Amos and Andy we weren't, but it was fun—and a kind of experience you couldn't learn in a classroom.

I pulled a self-styled version of The Sting in Peoria. It was a real con job. A phony poll.

Ever since, I've been suspicious of ratings, although I've benefited from them greatly over the years.

It was the era of Bradley's "Famous Five"—a classy collection of ball-handling magicians who were to elevate the small Peoria school into a major basketball power. They were six, actually—

Chuck Orsborn, Ted Panish, Dar Hutchins, Carl Schunk, Les Getz and Kenny Olson.

Basketball has changed considerably, but I still would rank that team as one of the 10 best in collegiate history.

Their coach and athletic director was the beloved A. J. Robertson. He was a shrewd judge of talent. He realized the potential of this team when they were underclassmen and began switching from a small-time to a big-time schedule.

I was anxious to broadcast Bradley basketball and Bradley was anxious to have me do it, but WMBD's front office frowned on it. As a CBS outlet, we were committed to such shows as Eddie Cantor, Kate Smith and Rudy Vallee.

In short, there wasn't room for basketball in prime time.

So program director Harold Bean and I decided to attempt to sell the idea of recording the games and playing them back late at night. This in itself was revolutionary because the station didn't own recording equipment.

We had a meeting with the brass and I was asked: "Who will pay attention to a game when they already know how it came out?"

I answered: "Let's take a poll and ask the people in Peoria how they feel about it."

That seemed sensible. However, the front office made one mistake. They let *me* conduct the poll.

I went to the corner of Main and Jefferson and threw this question at a total of ten people: "Would you be interested in listening to delayed broadcasts of Bradley basketball games, late at night, even though you probably already knew the final score?"

Eight answered "no"—they wouldn't be interested.

Two were undecided.

I threw those ballots in the sewer and raced to the rear-end of my favorite pool hall.

In the semi-darkness, I filled out 100 ballots.

I marked 62 ballots "yes" and 14 "no." The rest were undecided.

I took the phony poll to the station and on the basis of the big lie they agreed to try one broadcast.

I'll never forget it.

With equipment borrowed from a recording hobbyist in town, equipment which weighed roughly 200 pounds and caused the courtside table at the Peoria Armory to sag, we transcribed the Bradley-Louisville game on huge discs. Bradley won big.

During the broadcast, I mentioned frequently: "I know that as you listen to this, you probably know how the game came out. But because of network commitments, this is the only way we can bring you these games. Let us know if you want us to continue."

None of us was prepared for the response.

We broke the station's record for mail in a 48-hour period.

Petitions poured in from Caterpillar Tractor and Hiram Walker's and Keystone Steel and Wire and various service organizations. They said they loved it—and there was nothing phony about it this time.

It got to be a custom for fans to go to the games and then run home to turn on the radio and determine whether Brickhouse broadcast it the way they had seen it. This led to a full scheduling of delayed broadcasts.

And later, when Bradley went west to play teams like California and Nebraska, and won a bid to its first post-season tournament at Madison Square Garden, WMBD pre-empted the network and handled those games live.

As time went on, it became fashionable in Peoria to hold basketball-listening parties. For the first time, the station's call letters made the front page and society page as well as the sports page.

The Peoria Water Works was one of our sponsors. Peoria had its share of distilleries and breweries, so gagsters liked to say the Water Works needed the advertising because it was the one city where they had competition.

In December of 1938, after I had returned from a road trip with Bradley, the people at WMBD chipped in and bought me a watch. It was inscribed: "To Jack Brickhouse from the WMBD staff, 1938." They said it was in gratitude for promoting the image of the station.

To get this sort of memento for anything other than a farewell gift is most touching.

It meant the world to me.

Among a myriad of memories from my Peoria days, two more demand recounting.

It was a momentous occasion for Peoria in the 1930s when the great John Barrymore arrived to appear in *My Dear Children.* I wangled the assignment to interview Barrymore in his suite at the Pere Marquette Hotel, where WMBD had installed a line for just such purposes.

There was one hitch: I found Barrymore totally inebriated.

I was extremely apprehensive. This was to be a live interview.

His press agent assured me Barrymore would handle the questions properly. I took him at his word.

As a young product of Peoria's pool halls, I never had seen a stage play. I knew Barrymore only from his movies.

So my first question to this world-famous member of the First Family of American Theatre went like this: "Mr. Barrymore, before you got into the movies, were you ever on stage?"

Barrymore almost sobered up. He glared at me in that Barrymore way and snarled: "Ask me that again. Ask me that again, young man, and I can promise you my answer will cost your station its broadcasting license."

But the longest 15 minutes in my Peoria career came during an interview with a mounted policeman, one of a handful who had just been equipped with a police radio.

I stood on the curb, the cop stayed on his horse and I used my long reach, arm outstretched, to manipulate that microphone back and forth.

But I still wonder what that horse had eaten before he got there.

I simply couldn't quit in the middle of a live interview but as I told the man at the cleaners later, it was a messy situation.

It was 1940 when the telegram came. I still have it framed on the wall. The message was terse:

"Expect call from WGN regarding job as staff announcer and sports assistant. Remember, if asked, you have a thorough knowledge of baseball. Best regards. Bob Elson."

With that wire, Elson paved the way for me to join WGN. You need that little boost in our business, regardless of your talent, and Elson gave it to me. I auditioned and was hired by Quin Ryan.

And the rest has been the most pleasant relationship any man could ask for with any company.

II

"The Commander"

Through the years, I always cherished my friendship with Bob Elson. He was the master, a prototype of sorts, and without doubt the most imitated baseball broadcaster in history.

You can listen to tapes of lots of announcers around the country and hear a little of the Elson-type delivery whether they realize it or not.

Elson had a patented way of describing an otherwise routine out on a ground ball to the infield. "Heeeeez outtt," Elson would say, and you would know, for sure and certain, that the runner was out.

Elson goes back to the era of the 1930s in the day and age when five powerful radio stations carried the Cubs' games at the same time with pretty much the same sponsors.

The stations didn't even pay rights charges to the Cubs in those days. Baseball franchises were happy just to have the exposure.

Elson long insisted that Ted Husing was the best football announcer ever, Mel Allen and some guy from Peoria the best in baseball, and Lloyd Pettit the best in hockey.

I have insisted that among the old-timers, Pat

Flanagan was the best salesman of the baseball broadcasters, Hal Totten the best reporter, and Elson the best entertainer. I always have considered Husing the best all-around announcer, period.

But I'll make one thing perfectly clear: on a given baseball broadcast, for example a big Friday night in Yankee stadium when Billy Pierce of the White Sox was matched against Whitey Ford of the Yankees, you show me a man who could do a better job than Bob Elson.

There is none.

And it always amazed me that Elson's pleasant, melodious voice never changed one bit despite a half-century behind the mike.

Elson's reputation as a gin rummy shark and practical joker became somewhat legendary.

They still tell the story of the week he spent in vaudeville with Dizzy Dean at the old Palace theatre in Chicago. Elson brought along a World Series film, Diz commented on it, and for this kind of act the theatre paid Elson $1,000 and Dean $1,500.

But once they got paid off, Elson rushed for a deck of cards and parted Diz from his money in a matter of hours.

Elson gained considerable notoriety for his talented work on "Bob Elson on the 20th Century Limited." He would interview people leaving Chicago for New York on that great train and his line of questioning was super.

But he almost caused an international incident one day in a lull between interviews at Union Station.

A Swedish prince was visiting Chicago. Elson

called the secretary to the prince at the Ambassador Hotel and pretended to be the editor of the *Chicago Defender*, David Kellum.

"We represent 400,000 black readers in Chicago," snarled Elson, "to say nothing of our circulation in Louisville and Pittsburgh. I demand to know why I was not invited to the prince's press conference."

The secretary was startled. Elson continued, "I demand a press conference of my own with the prince. And when I get it, I want to ask him one question: 'If Sweden was so neutral in World War II, how come they sold all those ball bearings to Germany?' "

Elson had really touched a nerve.

Now there was flurried activity as the Swedish delegation tried to head off a blast in the *Defender*.

I heard later the State Department even got involved.

All because Elson had a spare moment or two.

Then there was the day in Iowa City when Illinois was playing Iowa in football, and I was doing the broadcast. But I was hopping mad. The hotel accommodations were crappy, even though I had made reservations three months earlier.

They had put our crew, four of us, in one room by providing a couple of seedy folding cots to go with two small beds.

The bathroom was down the hall. Further raising my ire was the fact that Fred Leo, then with WMBD, told me he had a comfortable suite with a parlor — and he had made reservations only three days before.

Elson was working the game with Red Grange for another Chicago station at this time, and Grange overheard me complaining in loud tones to the hotel manager's secretary about the shabby treatment. He tipped off Elson and as I returned to my room, I received the inevitable phone call.

"This is George Davis, the hotel manager," said the voice. "I understand you have a problem."

Whereupon I let him have it but good.

"You must understand," the voice droned, "that we are very crowded and very busy, so you can take the room or leave it."

I immediately threatened to complain to Eric Wilson, the athletic director at the University of Iowa. With that, the voice shouted: "You can tell Eric Wilson to go to hell."

I was infuriated. I slammed the receiver.

A moment later, another call. "This is George Davis again," he said. "I've been thinking it over and I've decided to take one dollar off your bill."

I told him what he could do with his dollar.

Later, at the tail end of my broadcast, I laid it on the hotel for its utter lack of hospitality.

Two days later, I attended a broadcasting luncheon in Chicago. Elson was there. "What have you heard from George Davis?" he inquired, with that Elson leer. I knew I had been had.

The late Vince Garrity, for years a loyal city employee, once told me of the night he was invited to accompany Elson on a speaking junket some 50 miles out of Chicago.

"Why not go along and keep me company?" offered Bob. "All you have to do is introduce me at the banquet. I don't know what they're paying but whatever it is we'll split 50-50."

I emphasize that Garrity and Elson each respected the other's cunning.

Garrity made a fine introduction and while Elson was speaking, the dinner chairman called Garrity aside and said: "Please give this envelope to Mr. Elson when he's through with his talk. His fee is in there."

Garrity retired to the men's room and opened the envelope. It contained $150 in cash. Vince stuck $50 in his pocket.

As Elson finished his speech, Garrity handed him the envelope. "It's your fee," he said.

Now Elson retired to the men's room and opened the envelope. It contained $100 in cash. Bob stuck $50 in his pocket.

Then he returned to Garrity's side, the envelope still in hand, took $25 out of it and handed it to Vince. "Here's your half," moaned Elson. "Let's get the hell out of here. The dirty bums only gave us $50."

A classic example of the double double cross. But beautiful.

The first big league game I ever worked with Elson came on a crowded Sunday at Wrigley Field in 1940. The booth was jammed, too, mainly because Elson was some kind of hypochondriac and usually invited a couple of doctors and nurses to join him in the booth.

Elson advised me to go sit in the press box. "Tell them I said it's all right. Then come back and do the seventh inning."

So I marched briskly into the press box, big as life and twice as smart. I was completely unaware that it was for newspapermen only, a fact of life traditionally protected zealously by members of the fourth estate.

Walter Johnson, the Andy Frain chief, stopped me. "Do you belong in here?" he inquired.

"Bob Elson said it was okay," I answered with self-assurance.

"You'll have to clear it with Irving Vaughan of the *Chicago Tribune*," offered Johnson. "He's in charge of the press box this season."

This posed no problem, I figured. After all, WGN and the *Chicago Tribune* were members of the same family. It would be merely routine, the formality of going through the motions.

I went up to Vaughan, offered a handshake with great joviality, and introduced myself. "I'm Jack Brickhouse, Mr. Vaughan. I'm working with Bob Elson at WGN now and he suggested I sit in here until the seventh inning. The Andy Frain man told me to clear it with you."

I later came to know Irving Vaughan as a highly-skilled professional writer, but at this moment he was a dour man with a fierce glare. "You tell Mr. Elson I do not send my guests down to his booth," he snapped, "and I would appreciate it if he didn't send his to the press box."

I hastened back to Elson and gave him the story. Elson just giggled as only Elson could giggle. He knew all along that veteran baseball writers of that era carried a built-in distrust of sports announcers. I had been fed to the lions.

There was the day in the long ago when I sat with two prominent advertising men in the Wrigley Building restaurant. This was in my pre-credit card life and it dawned on me that I didn't have enough cash in the event I wound up with the tab.

I spotted Elson several tables away. I went over and asked him to let me have twenty dollars until the next day. Elson gave it to me.

I returned to my table, secure in the knowledge I could handle the check. Five minutes later, Elson came by and in a loud voice asked: "Have you got that twenty I loaned you?"

I was embarrassed. "I told you I'd pay you tomorrow," I said, almost in a whisper.

Elson, speaking even louder now, warned: "Okay, you bum, but don't get hit by a bus." And he walked off, giggling.

Bob Elson was on the receiving end at times, too.

I remember the night Dick McNeeley got even. He used to write Elson's 6:15 sports review for radio and his scripts were works of art.

But Elson always would show up at the studio five seconds before air time, read a story or two from the script, then toss it aside and ad lib the rest of the show.

On this particular evening, Elson arrived in

the studio at the last second again, sat down in his chair in front of the mike, and grabbed the script. He had just started to say, "Good evening, this is Bob Elson," when he spotted a live seal sitting on the other side of the table.

It was Sharkey, the famous seal from the Sportsman's Show, and McNeeley had worked a deal with Sharkey's trainer just to shock Elson. Sharkey made all those typical seal noises even as Elson, visibly shaken, tried to bluff his way through the show. The trainer finally emerged from the control room to rescue both Elson and the seal!

In his days at WJJD in Chicago, Elson used to tickle announcer Chuck Bill while he was on the air in an effort to break him up, or he would do cute little things like setting Bill's script on fire.

But Chuck Bill had his day.

First off, he recruited about 20 of Elson's buddies to come over to the studio to witness what was to me one of the greatest practical jokes ever. Mike Wallace was there, George Rich, Eddie Short and a number of others interested in seeing a radio "first."

Elson began his evening sports review.

All of us filed into the studio.

Elson kept talking—but he knew something was going on.

Then in she came.

Chuck Bill had hired a beautiful Japanese-Hawaiian stripper. She stood in front of Elson and proceeded to strip.

Elson went on giving the baseball scores, giant beads of perspiration on his forehead.

The stripper took off everything but her toenail polish.

To Elson's eternal credit, he finished that show. Years later, he told me: "Boy, would I like to have a tape of that show. I don't know to this day what I said."

I nailed Elson one time.

He was doing radio and I was doing television at Comiskey Park. A thin wall separated our booths. It was easy to hear the other man's commentary.

I always prided myself in digging up human interest anecdotes and at that time, Bob Foster used to help me do it. Foster later became head of WGN's Washington Bureau.

In any case, I knew from various reports that Elson would pick off one of my items here and there, what with the thin wall and all, and report it as his own.

So I framed him one afternoon.

I cut my mike for a moment, so what I said didn't go out on the air, and in firm tones announced: "Here's a bulletin from WGN Sports. Phil Wrigley, head of baseball's 'Find a Commissioner Committee,' has just announced that at the next meeting of baseball's brass, Les O'Connor, former assistant to Judge Landis, and general manager of the White Sox, will be named to succeed lame duck commissioner Happy Chandler as commissioner of baseball."

Then I released the switch on the mike and went on doing the ball game.

Moments later, I could hear Elson report: "Here's a bulletin from the WJJD newsroom. Phil Wrigley has announced that at the next meeting of baseball's brass, my old and dear friend Les O'Connor, one of the greatest men in baseball history, will be named commissioner of baseball."

Whereupon Elson then spent several minutes building brownie points on behalf of his old pal, Les O'Connor.

Les didn't get the job and Elson never mentioned the incident to me.

As I look back, those really were happy days — they were times of few formalities, lots of hard work, and lots of laughs. Obviously, Elson was a man for his time. He belongs to the ages now. I miss him today and always.

III

"Live from the Marigold"

Hardly had WGN Television gone on the air in 1948 when I was summoned to the office of Frank Schreiber, the big boss.

I'm assigning you to telecast professional wrestling," said Frank. "It has tremendous potential."

I put up a beef. "What about my image as a legitimate sports announcer? Frank, you know as well as I that pro wrestling is a sham, a fake. It's hippodrome. Do me a favor—let me take a pass on this one."

So we compromised. I did wrestling.

There are those who say wrestling made me as a broadcaster by spreading my name throughout the Midwest and East in television's embryonic stages.

There are those who say I made pro wrestling the popular feature it was to become.

I reserve further comment on either contention.

I do know that wrestling on television repeatedly got ratings of 50 and better. Anything less than that was considered a slow night.

Wrestling in early television was one of the most spectacular and dramatic happenings to come along in the history of mankind's enjoyment of sports.

The new box with the magic eye was a natural for wrestling.

In those days, we were convinced there were two types of people: those who watched wrestling on television—and those who watched but wouldn't admit it.

Originally, I telecast wrestling three nights per week—from Marigold, on Chicago's North Side; from Madison Arena, on the West Side, and from Midway, on the South Side.

Marigold became the big deal. The Saturday night shows from there were carried on the DuMont Network.

But once the major networks started operating efficiently between New York and Chicago—they hadn't reached the West Coast yet—I figured the big entertainment shows would knock wrestling out of the box.

Wrong again.

Wrestling grew as a feature. Like Topsy. Station after station joined our network from Marigold. The bonanza spread eastward. Wrestling names became household words.

From a television standpoint, wrestling's heyday lasted nine years. I lasted all nine.

And with a show I hadn't wanted to do in the first place.

To this day, my respect for pro wrestlers is unlimited.

They are smart and they are shrewd, maybe more so than athletes in any other pro sport. They know they are paid to entertain and they do just that.

Wrestling's lexicon, in itself, was enough to

intrigue me. The various holds got wild names. The claw. The sleeper. The cobra twist. The Boston crab. The chicken wing. The step-over-toehold. The arm drag and whip. The figure 4 leglock. The piledriver.

If I didn't know the name of a particular hold, I made one up.

So did Wayne Griffin, who was telecasting a wrestling show on ABC at that time.

It was all part of wrestling's mystique.

Wrestling fans are a hard-core group, a cult. I have encountered many old-timers over the years who are unaware that I broadcast baseball and football. They know me only for my work on wrestling.

I found wrestling at the professional level to be simply a game of hero vs. villain, good guy vs. bad guy, almost like cops and robbers. They called the hero-type a "babyface" in the dressing room. It was his job to prove right over evil. He usually did.

Actually, I got the feeling a villain could make more money in the ring because more people would pay to boo than to cheer in the unique world of wrestling.

Such a villain was Hans Schmidt.

I have interviewed thousands of people, from presidents to skid row bums, from potentates to prostitutes, yet the interview which drew the greatest response was the one with Hans Schmidt at Marigold on a Saturday night in the early fifties.

Schmidt was the meanest, orneriest villain of his day, a villain's villain.

He looked the part of a German hangman. He was strong and he knew how to wrestle.

He had stomped "babyfaces" all over America. Fans had paid tens of thousands of dollars at the box office in the hope of being there when Schmidt got his comeuppance.

On this night, Hans Schmidt made the following statements to me on network television:

"I am going to win the title and take it back to Germany where it belongs. I will never give an American a crack at it.

"People who teach sportsmanship to their children are crazy. The only answer is to win at any cost.

"I don't like the fans. As a matter of fact, I hate them."

I had heard enough. I finally brought an end to this hammy interview in this manner:

"I cannot let this interview continue, Hans. You are violating everything I have been taught to hold dear. I only hope you get yours someday and when you do, that our cameras will be there to show it."

Within 48 hours, WGN received some 5,000 letters and telegrams, all but a handful violently protesting Schmidt's attitude.

Several psychiatrists offered to treat him for free.

Clergymen of every faith wanted to consult with Hans and try to save his obviously lost soul.

Undertakers from three cities said they would bury him for nothing.

The American Legion and VFW and Amvets wanted his hide.

And Adlai Stevenson was governor of Illinois then. He got all kinds of heat. That caused a stirring at the Illinois Athletic Commission.

The German-American newspaper in Chicago was upset. It felt Hans was besmirching the image of the German people just when there was a cooling off period in the wake of World War II.

The attorney general of the United States received calls demanding Schmidt's deportation as an undesirable alien.

The FBI dispatched an agent, Gus Kayne, to visit me and check out the whole story.

What Kayne learned was this:

Hans Schmidt was not a German at all. He was a French-Canadian and his real name was Guy LaRose. I doubt he could have found Germany on the map.

It seems Guy LaRose had failed to draw well as a wrestling attraction in Minneapolis. So his promoter there said: "You don't look French and you don't look Canadian. You look more like a German hangman. From now on, you're a German villain and your name is Hans Schmidt."

Schmidt's sudden notoriety paid off. He headed the card at Syracuse and pulled in a $15,000 house. They had been averaging $3,000.

Erie and Des Moines had turnaway crowds to see Hans Schmidt.

Schmidt subsequently returned to television with a written apology. He sneered: "I have been asked to apologize for my recent remarks. So I apologize."

Then he ripped the written apology to bits for all to see!

Schmidt became a $100,000 per year wrestler.

It didn't take me long to discover that professional wrestling was theatrical rather than phony. For instance, if you were to apply a full nelson on me face down, or a good headlock, you could hold it all night long and people would stay away from the box office by the thousands. To attract the entertainment dollar, it was mandatory for the pros to introduce theatrics. That they did.

But virtually every one of the top pros was a stand-out wrestler and absorbed a certain amount of punishment, win or lose.

The fact that one wrestler might be told to lose in order to build up another wrestler was strictly a box office maneuver. After all, there was no betting involved, so no one got hurt in that area.

I'm not here to discuss the morals of such thinking, just the realities.

I found that wrestling gave a dollar's entertainment for every dollar spent by the fan—and I defy Hollywood or Broadway or other sports to make that statement every time out.

As the announcer, I was part and parcel of the whole scene. If the villain applied a headlock, I had the ability to make it sound barbaric. If the hero applied that same hold, I made it sound scientific.

The big promoters were something else. Fred Kohler. Jim Barnett. Pinky George. Great names in their field. Kohler undoubtedly was the best wrestling promoter who ever lived. He was the first to take advantage of the benefits of televised wrestling. And Bob Luce, who learned his lessons well under Kohler, later moved into promotional prominence.

Yes, I have fond memories of my wrestling associations. I remember especially Rudy Kay and Al Williams, and the Schnabel brothers, Hans and Fritz. They were tough and clever and entertaining, and fun to be around.

I remember the night at Marigold I showed up at my ringside mike wearing a suit the color of vanilla ice cream. Kay and Williams worked up a good sweat and then took turns throwing each other into my lap. Soon my suit was charcoal. After that, I telecast from the first row of the balcony.

Kay and Hans Schnabel body slammed each other so hard so many times one night they broke the floor of the ring. That was no put on.

There was Gentleman Jim Dobie. He overcame polio in his boyhood and went on to wrestling fame. And he spent hundreds of hours in hospitals encouraging other polio victims to keep up the fight.

Gypsy Joe Dorsetti was somewhat of a philosopher. "Dey been tryin' to stamp out rasslers for four thousand five hunnert years," he exclaimed one night, "But we're still around."

Verne Gagne and television were made for each other.

Gagne came out of the Northlands and fit the Paul Bunyan mold.

He had played football at the University of Minnesota. He had won four Big 10 wrestling championships in various weight classifications.

Physique. Good looks. Charisma. Gagne had it all. And Kohler, in his shrewdness, recognized Verne's potential immediately, if not sooner.

I recall Gagne's first pro match in Chicago opposite champion Lou Thesz. Kohler made this forecast: "If Gagne makes any kind of showing against Thesz on television tonight, he'll become one of the great ones."

Verne fought the great Thesz to a one-hour draw that night and became an overnight sensation.

Gagne always philosophized that a wrestler comes to know within himself whether he deserves the role of good guy or bad guy—and sometimes, he opined, the realization of this fact of life might take two or three years. I don't know about that. All I know is that Gagne was a good guy from the go. A real Mr. Clean.

Verne and I still talk about the night he was booked into Madison Square Garden and I was hired as guest ring announcer. The Garden had been drawing crowds of 3,000 and 4,000 for wrestling. The night we were there, some 18,000 showed up.

I'd like to think I was responsible for a small portion of that huge turnout. Even if I wasn't, it is pleasurable to relate that one pretty female fan came up to me and cut off a lock of my hair for a souvenir. I don't have enough hair left these days to allow that sort of thing.

In any case, Verne and I got a police escort and the whole bit that night in the Garden. It was terribly exciting.

In my mind, even now, Verne Gagne remains a superstar in the world of wrestling, the sport's most successful figure ever, a man completely unaffected by his staggering accomplishments in athletics and business.

Then there was Morris Shapiro. He called himself the Mighty Atlas and advertised himself as wrestling's strongest man. He very well could have been just that.

The Mighty Atlas had gimmicks. He would tie one end of a rope to a car bumper, put the other end of the rope in his mouth and pull the car down the street of a small town in order to build up the gate that night.

He would bend a crowbar into a shamrock.

And he would lie on his back in the ring, put a bed of spikes against his chest, put an anvil atop the spikes and let a couple of customers get up out of the audience and pound on the anvils with sledge hammers. How he tolerated it I'll never know.

Atlas kept a small bottle of rubbing alcohol at ringside in case the spikes broke his skin. This one night, he went through the sledge hammer routine, jumped up to the tumultuous applause, then reached for the alcohol. One problem: the cap was sticky and he couldn't get it off, try as he may.

Here was wrestling's strong man, unable to unscrew a cap from a small bottle. A few of the customers at ringside noticed. They snickered. Then they laughed. Now the first 10 rows were laughing.

The Mighty Atlas was enraged. He gave the bottle one furious look and threw it the length of the hall, then stomped off to the dressing room!

Then there was Jules LaRance. Rough and mean-looking and very hairy. I had received a letter from a female viewer wanting to know where

Jules stayed when he wrestled in Chicago. He gave me the okay to broadcast it.

"Ordinarily, I do not answer this type of mail publicly," I announced, "but since Jules has approved it, I will tell this young lady that when he is in Chicago, Jules stays at the Chelsea Hotel on Wilson Avenue."

One week later, I saw LaRance at another show. He grumbled: "I'll never tell you nothin' again. I ain't had 10 minutes sleep all week."

The reason was obvious: dozens of women had called Jules at various hours of the day and night. He finally had to plug his phone. "A lot of dese dames gave me the old story," said LaRance. "They could see me in the afternoon but not at night because they were livin' with their father or keepin' house for their brother. They weren't foolin' me a bit."

Among wrestling's VIPs is the man they call The Carpenter. He's the preliminary-type wrestler, generally an old-timer, whose job is to build a young prospect into solid box-office material. You know, maybe go one fall, a 20-minute time limit opening bout, and give his opponent all sorts of opportunities to look good.

The Carpenter may be obliged to lose to his opponent but there is no law in the land which says he must respect him. The young prospect probably is getting more money and more publicity anyhow, and these factors have a tendency to create jealousy.

I used to see cases where The Carpenter would mete out plenty of punishment to his young foe before losing in a huff, and the classic example was delivered by Johnny Carlin, a ring veteran in Sweden even before coming to America 30 years earlier.

What hair Johnny Carlin had left was dyed, he had scar tissue on top of scar tissue, his eyes were slits, his ears were cauliflower. He had been through the mill.

And here at Marigold this night, Johnny was matched against a handsome, well-built, agile, young man who appeared to be a cinch for future stardom.

Carlin, playing his role as The Carpenter to the hilt, maneuvered himself to his hands and knees and allowed the kid to get behind him and apply various holds. But the boy wonder got excited by the full house and the television cameras and all and suddenly he let Johnny have it smack in the face with his knee. It was vicious and you could hear Johnny Carlin's nose pop all over the hall, broken maybe for the 25th time.

Now you could see a flash in Carlin's old eyes —and for the next 15 minutes, a man gave a lesson to a boy, the most memorable demonstration of its kind I've ever seen in any sport.

Every time the boy wonder turned around, Carlin hit him with a fist, an elbow, a foot, a knee or a head. In the nose, the eye, the mouth, the groin, the ear. The kid was bleeding from every pore.

Just before the bell, Johnny Carlin applied a choke hold and was disqualified.

But he had gotten across his message.

Fred Kohler once told me the story of Miguel Torres, the Mexican wrestling villain, who aroused the fans in Mexico one night by practically destroying the local hero one bone at a time.

Tempers erupted to a point where Miguel needed a police escort to his dressing room.

The police were unhappy with Miguel, too. One jostled him en route to the clubhouse. Miguel responded with a forearm across the cheek. The policeman responded by raising his rifle and shooting Miguel in the arm.

The promoter's assistant raced into the counting house yelling: "The policia. The policia. They have just shot Miguel!"

The promoter rubbed his hands and grinned: "Ah, good finish, good finish!"

IV

On Broadcasting and Broadcasters

I can list thousands of people I'd rather debate than Howard Cosell. He's a word factory with a steel-trap mind. He never will use a two-syllable word where a four-syllable word will do. Howard Cosell could write his own dictionary and even Webster somehow would find a way to come back and smile his approval. I have found myself on opposite sides of the fence from Howard on countless occasions, yet I have discovered he's a refreshing sort even when he commandeers a cocktail party with that swashbuckling way of his. I sometimes get the feeling he ought to go around in one of those outfits the buccaneers wore on the high seas.

In any event, Howard Cosell and I met head-to-head on Kup's Show—and what a fantastic job Irv Kupcinet turns in consistently—on WMAQ-TV, the NBC outlet in Chicago, in October of 1974. Some said later that I came out ahead but they are my closest friends and frankly, I doubt that anyone tops Howard. He's something else. A transcript of most of the repartee follows:

Kup: I wonder, Howard, if you'd like to explain what your philosophy is, the "tell it like it is" philosophy, and see where you and Jack may have some differences on the role of the sportscaster; legitimate and honest differences.

Cosell: Well, I think what you're really trying to pinpoint, rather than going into general philosophy on this show, is the fact that Jack is a play-by-play announcer for a Chicago team and is a member of the Board of Directors of that team— and I do not adhere to the notion that this is fitting and proper from a point of view of journalism. It has nothing to do with Jack individually. He's a man I've known for many years and I like and respect him. But I don't think it's good for our profession to have that situation exist and quite evidently the Federal Communications Commission agrees with me because they've just enforced a new rule pursuant to an investigation inspired by an astute young reporter, Mike Roberts of the *Washington Star-News*, which requires that such affiliations be disclosed so that there can be no pretense of journalism. My fundamental philosophy is that sports is part of life, must be treated just as any other part of life is in the reportage of it.

Kup: Jack, do you feel that this is a slight at the Jack Brickhouse School of Broadcasting?

Brickhouse: Well, I'm going to echo what Howard said in the business of liking each other personally because we have known each other for a long time and I've watched Howard come up and I've admired him and I have a great respect for Howard's act. I'm going to call it an act, Howard, just because I also have an act. I don't mean this in any super-critical manner. So I don't know if we're trying to pinpoint whether or not I should be a member of the Board of Directors of the Chicago Cubs as an issue because I have to think that nothing could be less important really when it comes to broadcasting. The reason that I'm a member of the Board of Directors of the Chicago Cubs — and I didn't really expect this to be brought into the conversation this heavily, or this quickly at least, or as an issue — is because I happen to be a very dear friend of the Chicago Cubs, a great fan of the Chicago Cubs, a great admirer and friend of the Wrigley family. And consequently, Phil Wrigley once said there was an opening on his Board and it occurred to him that maybe it might not be a bad idea to have somebody on that Board who does actually live with that ball club day-in and day-out on the road, who gets close to those players and who can represent a little different viewpoint than we'll say very often the members of the Board of Directors of a giant corporation represent. I might add that it pays nothing, I own one share of stock in the Wrigley Company, rather in the Chicago Cubs, and that was my idea because I just figured that maybe as a member of the board I should have a share of stock. I bought it for $431 and I think I could sell it at a profit, but they haven't paid a dividend, I don't think, since 1945 with this stock.

Kup: But you do get all the free gum you can chew, don't you?

Brickhouse: No, the two are divorced totally, absolutely and totally divorced. And that, incidentally, is a very, very strong matter of policy where Mr. Wrigley is concerned. The gum company is publicly owned and the ball club is almost privately owned, you know, because he has so much of the stock. But can you imagine anybody, in your wildest imagination, saying: "I don't believe that Ernie Banks hit a home run because the guy who just said so is a member of the board of the Cubs and he has a vested interest?"

Cosell: No, I can't imagine that, Jack.

Brickhouse: Now, the FCC thing, Howard, first of all, they haven't come to any serious conclusions on that one yet. I have yet to be approached by anybody from the FCC. I understand they have communicated with my company. I am in the employ, incidentally, of WGN Continental Broadcasting Company, not the Cubs or anybody like that. So I think the disclaimer they are talking about....

Cosell: That will not apply to you since you're being paid by the station. It will apply to those who are paid by the clubs, and a very goodly number are paid by the clubs, as you know.

Brickhouse: I've been in both situations. I once worked for the New York baseball Giants and they paid the announcers. But most of the time I've always worked for the station itself, which I consider the best way to approach broadcasting. But I don't think this is that serious an issue. I think that, after all, we're in the entertainment business. I don't think the future of civilization rests on whether Oakland wins the championship.

Cosell: You say we're in the entertainment business, Jack. I've been reading the splendid minds of the sporting press, many of them, not all, over the recent four years I've watched a phenomenon called Monday Night Football grow, and I've watched many of these good and tried and true men tell us that it's entertainment, not football. Let me tell you something. If it weren't entertainment, there would be no Monday Night Football in prime time.

Brickhouse: Well, in that case, we're on the same wavelength.

Cosell: Yes, sports are entertainment. But there are great issues in sports that relate to the realities of life. They happen every single day. In every walk of life. A case of his friend and mine, Muhammad Ali, is just one evidence of that. There was a noticeable tendency upon the part of most sportscasters, certainly at the national level, to shy away from that issue and take the easy and popular way out. There were great issues that arose during the recent two Olympiads. There are many other great issues. Obviously, Monty Moore, whom I don't even know—and I'm sure he's a very nice and a very professional man—can't say anything that would stir up Mr. Finley of the Oakland A's. He'd get fired if he said so-and-so did something wrong. It has happened. Jim Woods was fired out of that very city.

Brickhouse: If it goes that far, you're right, Howard.

Cosell: And it does go that far in many cases.

Brickhouse: Not in my life, and I can only speak for Jack Brickhouse, of course.

Cosell: Fine, Jack, and I agree with that. That's an individual case. But you see, when I decry your position as a director on the board, it has no relevancy to you as an individual. You know me well enough to understand that.

Brickhouse: I understand.

Cosell: Nor does the fact that you've never gotten a dime from them as a director or anything else really have any relevancy. What does have relevancy is that factually, as a matter of law, it creates a conflict of interest that is bad as a matter of principle for our profession. I don't want anybody to say broadcasters are shills. And that has happened repeatedly in my 18 years as a sports broadcaster. To all of us. And that's true, you know it.

Brickhouse: You're going to get the rap no matter what. But why take it so seriously? This is entertainment, Howard. We get enough tragedy, we get enough sadness at the top of the news or on the front page of the paper. I take the position that we can overdo the theory that sports has great issues that are relevant to our civilization and to our times and our future. I don't think we should drag sports into that category. Sports is an escape from the seriousness and the intensities of that category we're talking about.

Cosell: Well, those are the utterances of the Bowie Kuhns and the Pete Rozelles of the world and . . . .

Brickhouse: I wouldn't exactly call them morons, would you?

Cosell: Well, I wouldn't exactly call Bowie Kuhn a genius.

Brickhouse: Well, he's a lawyer.

Cosell: That's hardly an evidence of intelligence.

Kup: That's the condemnation of all time, Jack.

Brickhouse: Aren't you a lawyer, Howard?

Cosell: Yes, I'm a lawyer. And I'd like to go into a courtroom against my good friend, Bowie. But you see, sports has projected itself into every walk of life. Sports in the contemporary society is big business and I find it a rather Neanderthal copout to say, "It's our escape, whatever happens there is fine and let's just give the games and all the rest." Because, you see, when baseball owners in the sport that you most love carpetbag all over this country, defy populations by abrupt removals, even as Chuck Finley would like to do with his Oakland A's, even as has happened to us in New York City. And on and on go the recitals. Milwaukee to Atlanta for a better TV. You're getting into a defiance of the public interest in the very thing that you proclaim nothing but an escape and a copout.

Brickhouse: Oh, don't make a guy moving a franchise sound like Watergate, Howard, for heaven's sake! Don't take it so seriously. Look, let me ask you something. If all the sports broadcasters and all the baseball owners and all the garbage collectors in the world were to go on strike at once, which one do you think would be missed first?

Cosell: The garbage collectors.

Brickhouse: Of course. Let's take it from there.

Cosell: That's exactly why I can't understand the whole sports motif. When the baseball players went on strike and the football players went on strike, all I ever read—and only Red Smith wrote and addressed himself to this issue on a national level—all I ever read was, "Hey! The fan wants the game. We don't care about the owners, we don't care about the players, give the fan his game." The fan IS a garbage collector and he has never given up the right to strike. The fan IS a power company worker. He has never given up the right to strike. The fan IS a teacher, a nurse. They have never given up the right to strike. And when any of them strike, it is clearly deleterious to the public safety and welfare. Yet, I find people in sports communications, broadcasters and writers alike, always saying, "Hey! Go back to work. You're taking away our pleasure." And they're supporting the alleged fan, the guy who never gave up his right. This is all interwoven in the complex structure of our society today, and it's why you can't oversimplify and reduce the issues involved in sports that relate to the realities of life by saying, "This is an Alice in Wonderland. Go through the looking glass. We just tell about Ernie Banks and so on."

Kup: Jack, let me bring this down to what I think Howard really says in his book. He says that the house speakers or the house announcers, as he calls them, the men who are maintained by the sports clubs themselves, and paid by the sports clubs, do not tell it like it really is. They will exaggerate the size of the crowd, or they won't tell the truth about the crowd, they won't tell the truth about fights on the field.

Cosell: Well, Red Barber got fired.

Kup: Red Barber got fired once for something along the same line. That's the point Howard makes. He even calls a farcical development the appointment of Jack Brickhouse to the Board of Directors of the Chicago Cubs.

Cosell: I didn't say it was a farcical development. I said it was wrong and I named Chick Hearn, who is a member of the board of the Los Angeles Lakers.

Brickhouse: Let's discriminate between play-by-play men and the color men, or the so-called studio sports announcer-reporter. There is a difference.

Cosell: That's absolutely true.

Brickhouse: Now the play-by-play man can be, if necessary, a color man or a studio commentator. He very often is. I would respectfully submit to you that the color man, though, is very unlikely to be a good play-by-play man because there's a basic talent involved here that you either have or you do not have. The basic talent is the ability to speak rapidly and be understood. This is the play-by-play man's job. What I'm getting at here is that this play-by-play fellow does not have an ax to grind. He is down there trying to call what he sees. Now this business of telling it like it is can bore me stiff for the very simple reason that there is a big difference sometimes between telling it like it is and telling it like you think it is. And I'm going to tell you, Buster, there's a big difference there. And I myself do not have the heart to sit in that booth and say that so-and-so was burned on a play, or made a mistake on a play, only to go down to the dressing room later and find out that he was trying to cover for the guy who made the original mistake. Now the retraction you make is like the retraction which is printed on page 38 of the newspaper the next day. It is lost. But the damage is done. An undeserving man has been hurt. For that reason, I would rather look for positives in broadcasting than negatives, even if you call it a copout. I would rather look for something nice to say. Howard, I still think that when you started out in this business, if somebody would have assured you right then and there that you could be twice as rich, and twice as powerful, and twice as well-known as you are today by being Mr. Nice Guy . . . . I'll bet butter wouldn't melt in your mouth.

Kup: Jack has made an accusation that you would be a different Howard Cosell if you could make as much money being a nice guy as you could being a critic.

Brickhouse: More money, twice as much.

Cosell: Jack doesn't know me.

Kup: That is a pretty damaging charge, I would say.

Cosell: I don't view it as a damaging charge at all. It's a statement made by Jack and it has no foundation whatsoever. And I'm not going to quarrel with Jack personally as anybody who knows me knows that that's simply not a possible way of life for Howard Cosell. I am now at the top of my game. I am what they call a hot commodity in show business. You know that, Kup. I make a lot of money and so on, yet I'm conjuring with the notion of leaving it. And I'm not that rich a man. I don't cotton to what Jack said at all, but I'm not going to quarrel with him about it. If that's his conviction, he's entitled to it. It's a free country. Jack Brickhouse, you know better. You really know better.

Brickhouse: I really don't know better, Howard.

Cosell: On the contrary, Jack, every step of the way I had to fight every trend in broadcasting to survive. For five years of my life I was blacklisted by the ABC Television Network, as I explained in my first book, because I was controversial, because I would speak out.

Brickhouse: That's a gimmick, Howard. You are not the first man to do it.

Cosell: Who on a national level, Jack?

Brickhouse: I'll take you back to guys like Sam Balter and Cal Tinney and fellows like that who made a career out of doing it because they had a sponsor who demanded that it be done that way. I turned down that particular show myself at one time in my early career in radio.

Cosell: If you followed your thesis to its logical conclusion, you are saying that everybody can be bought. It's just not true.

Brickhouse: I didn't say that, Howard, just certain ones.

Cosell: I stand on that.

Brickhouse: Wait a minute, I'll stand on this. When you broke in, if you'd go on the air and say nice things about people, you would have been fifth in line behind the Curt Gowdys, the Chris Schenkels, the Lindsey Nelsons, fellows like that, the Bob Elsons and Mel Allens and maybe even a Jack Brickhouse here and there. So you're going to take a long time getting any place.

Cosell: Jack, I took a long time getting any place. I took 18 years. I took all kinds of vilification. I took, when I started Monday Night Football, sponsors who demanded that I be taken off the air. I was very fortunate to have a man like Roone Arledge to back me up. Yet you make it sound very easy. It's quite the converse.

Howard Cosell and I got together again the day after Kup's Show. At my invitation, he was kind enough to drop by the WGN Radio booth at Soldier Field to cut a tape before the Bears' Monday night game against Green Bay. Howard talked at length about the demands on his time in conjunction with Monday Night Football—his personal appearance schedule and all—but he emphasized his undying gratitude to the folks at ABC who had made the whole thing possible. He pointed out the difficulty in gathering and then ad libbing the halftime highlights and insisted this was the toughest phase of the operation. Then our conversation took this course:

Brickhouse: Howard, you and I are probably pretty different in our approach as to how sports should be covered. I believe that there probably is room for editorializing in sports but the way I look at it—and I want to get your response to this—is that too often we shoot off from the heart and not from the head. We shoot from the hip. We sit in the booth here and look down there and make judgments. As I see editorialization, you should research it. You should really dig. You should go through maybe sometimes a carload of mold in order to get a quart of penicillin. But when you lay out the facts, they should be indisputable. They are facts one, two, three, four and five from which you may then, on the basis of your knowledge and your experience and maturity and intelligence, draw some kind of logical conclusion.

Cosell: I agree in some respects with that. I disagree in others. I want to make it clear that I think you're a fine man, that I like you, and I respect you. The fact that we may have different opinions on our approach to the transmission of a contest is just another fact of American life and I don't deem it of monumental significance that we have disagreements in this regard.

With that as a backdrop and with regard to commentary or editorialization during the transmission of a contest, I think that journalism demands it. I don't think I ever have shot from the hip. I have lived a lifetime on the sports beat. I'm here self-relating. I'm not sure if that's what your question relates to, but I think ultimately it must. If a man doesn't know the players, every one of them, his life history, everything that he has been able to garner about the man from personal contact, questioning and association, everything about the sport from years of observation and experience, then he's not qualified. But if a man has done those things and lived a life with it, I think in this day and age, especially in the light of all of the great circumstances of contemporary life, when people have lived through three assassinations and an attempted fourth, when people have lived through the Watergate and the subversion of the Presidency, when people have lived through an overwhelming narcotics addiction all around us, when people have lived with a constancy of racial anguish, especially the young people, and they are the people who dominate our respective listenerships and viewerships, I think we fail in our duty, over publicly-owned airways and publicly-licensed stations, if we don't express opinions. Now you have told me you don't want to burn anybody, and you were alluding to a football contest, because in baseball you don't have the same situation.

Brickhouse: Not too often but you'll have it, like on a play at second base or something.

Cosell: Occasionally, then. But mainly in football, when a cornerback is apparently burned and when you would go down to the dressing room and have them tell you, "Hey! It wasn't his fault—he was trying to cover for the free safety, who missed the coverage." And so he shouldn't really have been blamed. And you say you don't want to be guilty of that. That's a detail in the fabric of what I'm talking about. It happens only rarely and I think that attitude very often, based upon my experience through all of the years, is falling prey to the mysteries created by the ex-athlete who invades broadcasting and by the sportswriters who never have played the game but who would like to cultivate the favor of those who have played the game by cottoning to them. I have scant respect for such people. I do not find the game mysterious. Really, the game was not invented by Enrico Fermi and refined by Werner von Braun. It really was not. I have listened to Bart Starr, who I think on any list of the world's great gentlemen has to be Number One, and I deem him a great friend of mine. I got him to go out, together with his wife, and live for three days at Carroll Rosenbloom's house relative to getting the job as coach of the Los Angeles Rams. I think John Unitas was the greatest quarterback I've ever seen. I think John Brodie is really a very nice fellow, who never had the team around him to win the big one but who is a very great quarterback. But if I hear them tell me one more time about isolating the setback, one-on-one against the linebacker . . . . why in 1924, when New York State had blue and white license plates, and they've never had them since, or that we sent the fast kid out against the slow kid . . . I don't want to hear that garbage any more. And that's part and parcel of what I call nonjournalism and I don't fault those people. They shouldn't be in my business. There is nothing in their backgrounds and their lives to qualify them for journalism, for immediacy of vocal communication, mass communicatively, and our business apart from prostitution is the only business, Jack Brickhouse, where a man can come in overnight because he played the game. And I think it's despicable and I will never concede to it, and I blame my industry, not the jocks. This is all in my new book, *Like It Is.* It couldn't be clearer. I don't want any part of it and I like and respect John Brodie, John Unitas and . . . .

Brickhouse: Freddie Williamson . . . .

Cosell: Freddie Williamson was totally unqualified. I think Alex Karras is doing a great job but I do not liken Karras to the jocks. We don't have him on the air to be a jock, to isolate the setback one-on-one against the linebacker, or talk about flooding the zone and clearing it out so you can throw to the wide receiver underneath. I'll tell you this about Alex Karras. The man is a born performer with a lot of performance experience. The man has got a great sense of humor and when you're on in prime time against Maude and Rhoda and the Monday Night Movie, one of which is *The Godfather*, if you're talking about isolating the set-back one-on-one against the linebacker, there's no Monday Night Football.

Brickhouse: Would you agree that there might be exceptions? For example, how would you have rated Paul Christman?

Cosell: Paul Christman I would have rated "A." The man had succinctness, he had fight, he had humor, he did not regard a contest on the gridiron as a religious service at St. Patrick's.

Brickhouse: How do you view your assignment?

Cosell: My own assignment is to control the booth, to be the catalyst in the booth, to provide human insight into the athletes to the fullest possible degree, for which, as you know, I'm eminently qualified because of all of the years on the beat and my personal associations with them, to quickly summarize that which has taken place, to embellish what my colleagues say. After all, when Frank Gifford, in the Bears' upset of the Vikings two years ago, had Eischeid kicking for both teams— and Gifford played the game—I found it necessary, up to a point, to studiously overlook it and then to make the point that he was right. Eischeid was a hell of a kicker and should have been kicking for both teams.

Brickhouse: How do you rate the various play-by-play men in your book?

Cosell: I don't like to get into that, not on grounds of chickening out, but because I've got a great number of friends. Let me say this: on the network level, I have a deep respect for Keith Jackson. It's not because he's a friend of mine but because he has worked so hard and knows his work so well. I also have a deep respect for Curt Gowdy. Here I could be disqualified on grounds of bias because he is my best friend in broadcasting.

Brickhouse: Can I gather some implications by the names you have not mentioned?

Cosell: No, I don't think that's fair.

Brickhouse: Do you have any fellows you think really don't belong there in the big time?

Cosell: I will only say this: I think most of them don't belong there.

Brickhouse: You have an outstanding command of rhetoric. I love the way you throw the language around, I really do. I know you make a lot of speeches. What would you say was the greatest speech you've ever delivered?

Cosell: I think they're all great, Jack. Oh, I'm just kidding. I don't think I can single out one speech. Every time you face a live audience, whether on campus or in industry, wherever, you have new challenges, new stimuli. I gave a speech a few weeks ago to kick off the United Way campaign in New Orleans. I'm very proud of that speech. I captured those people. I delivered a speech before the Yale Political Union, the Harvard Law Forum. I delivered a commencement speech at Wilmington College in Ohio where the Bengals train. I'm very proud of those speeches.

Brickhouse: Favorite coach?

Cosell: I think the best coach in football is Don Shula. I think the next great coach is Chuck Knox of Los Angeles.

Brickhouse: Do you feel yourself mellowing in the last year? Honestly, I think you have mellowed. I don't think you're as ornery as you were a year ago or two years ago.

Cosell: No, I don't agree with that. I don't think I've changed. I think perhaps it's the departure of Dandy Don Meredith. He had his own thing to do, his own ax to grind, a warm, decent, generous human being I always will love. We will always see one another. And in the nature of things — and it worked for the American public — Don was my adversary, presumably. And so it looked like I was abrasive and ornery and all the rest. I do not mean that I am kindly and sweet. It's not within me, except in my family life and in my feelings about people generally. But that's not in my broadcast personality. I really haven't mellowed. I do find a simpler situation in the booth this year with Alex Karras, and I think noticeably it has helped Frank Gifford, who is more relaxed and came to me and said that very thing. No other man could have said Barzilutski instead of Barzilauskas after an hour of rehearsal!

Brickhouse: Howard, we have to go to work, both of us.

Cosell: Jack, thank you.

Brickhouse: Welcome to Chicago, pal. Good luck.

I once told baseball player Kevin Joseph (Chuck) Connors to go by the name of Kevin Connors if he intended to make a career in show business. "The name Chuck Connors is too common. It won't catch on," I insisted.

And I advised Joe Garagiola, at the tail end of his baseball days, to stay with some phase of baseball and forget broadcasting. One day, on the air, Joe and I discussed my foresight. The interview went like this:

Garagiola: Jack, before you start questioning me, I understand you told Edison to forget the light bulb and Eli Whitney to forget the cotton gin—that the chances of success were slim.

Brickhouse: I must admit, Joe, that you are one of the jocks who has made it big in broadcasting. There has been a certain resentment by play-by-play announcers toward ex-athletes who have moved in. I don't share that resentment and I proved it long ago by recommending Lou Boudreau at WGN. What are your views on entry of the jock into broadcasting?

Garagiola: First of all, it bothers me that Howard Cosell, for example, has been on a soap box saying that the only thing the former athlete brings to the broadcast booth is mediocrity. I can't quarrel with that because if there's an expert on mediocrity, it is Cosell.

I think there's room for both the athlete and the non-athlete broadcaster in the same booth. I make no bones about it. The fact I was a baseball player got me the job. But that's not what keeps you there. I felt that if I worked hard and tried hard to improve myself I would be able to maintain that job.

I can understand the viewpoint of young broadcasters who work at small stations and do all kinds of play-by-play and sports shows. All of a sudden the network makes a move and hires a prominent athlete. If you were working at a small station, you'd say: "I'll never get the chance as long as they keep signing those ballplayers."

Yet, there's a specific need for an athlete according to the networks or according to the sponsors, and that's why they hire them.

It bothers me when athletes get the job and then stop doing the one thing for which they were hired—and that is to continue talking and thinking like an athlete. What makes a professional announcer? Do you want to match paychecks, do you want to match events that are covered? No, that's not it. The training you get makes you an announcer. The fact you weren't able to be a professional baseball player, for example, doesn't make you less knowledgeable about the game.

But I, Joe Garagiola, know what it's like to stand up there and take a third strike with the bases loaded. There's no way a Jack Brickhouse can know that feeling. Now Jack Brickhouse has trained himself to describe that feeling. But he can go only so far with words, then it's up to the ballplayer to jump in and say, "Well, here's the way I felt."

Maybe it's an oversimplification, Jack, but you come out to a ball park like Wrigley Field. There's no way an athlete can describe the beauty of this field, of this ball park, with the vines, with the breeze, with the clouds, with the sky, with the excitement, the intimacy of the fans in relationship to the field itself. No athlete can describe that like a non-athlete broadcaster.

But you're looking at it that way. I come out to Wrigley Field and I say, "Look at that wind blowin' in, the flag is blowin' in, that means the knuckle ball is gonna move."

You look at the grass and you see it's manicured beautifully and you describe it so well. I look at it and I say, "If I'm not careful that ball is gonna skip off that grass."

You look at the foul lines and you say the ground crew really did a great job and you build this beautiful word picture. I look at it and I say, "Those sonofaguns, they tilted the foul lines and that ball is gonna stay fair, so I better bust out of that catcher's box in a big, big hurry."

My point is that there doesn't have to be resentment because a man is a former athlete. I tend to be a dese, dose and dat's guy. I get excited. My thinking about broadcasting is that it should be like two guys are sitting at a ball park talking and there happens to be a microphone there and people eavesdropping.

When I come out to Wrigley Field to cover a game, I have an edge. I played the game and I can get to the ballplayers and agitate them. I've got to come here and smell the sweatshirts and get on the bench with the guys. I can't come here and sit in a press room, or I can't just say, "Well, I'm gonna go right up to the booth and I'll be ready to broadcast the game."

I feel the viewer is as much as saying to me, "Look, Joe, I worked hard all day and I can't get out to that ball park. They're paying you good money to get out there. You tell me how Ernie Banks feels. You tell me if Fanzone played a jazz concert the night before. You tell me how so-and-so's leg is. And so forth and so on."

It bothers me considerably—it's almost a thing with me—when I see the athlete who got the job because he was an athlete all of a sudden want to be a Jack Brickhouse or Mel Allen.

Brickhouse: I think this, Joe. I'm a professional broadcaster. I'm an announcer, schooled in the problems of cues, scripts and an instinct for what goes wrong. And . . . .

Garagiola: And word description, Jack. That's what makes a trained announcer. It's not just the technical things.

Brickhouse: All right, I'm the play-by-play guy, you're the color man. I think the best way to get the job done is for the play-by-play guy to be in control of that broadcast. Otherwise, you and I are going to be talking at the same time all the time. Let me call that play-by-play and take it so far, then bring in a Joe Garagiola and let him complete that picture.

If you've got something you think may fit, hold up that finger and I'll signal you to come in. But I have to be in charge—and if I'm smart, I'll play you like a harp and we'll have a good show.

Getting back to Howard Cosell, Joe, neither of us has any quarrel with ambition. But do you think that if Howard could be twice as big a man tomorrow and twice as successful by changing his image to Mr. Nice Guy that he would do it?

Garagiola: If he could—but I don't think he could. Monday Night Football has been his great thing. And it has really helped him and obviously it is successful. But there are certain non-athlete broadcasters whom I call Red Book and Green Book announcers—you know, those books handed out to the press by the league offices. This type of announcer says: "Here is Jack Brickhouse, 6-2. 210 pounds, went to Ohio State University, his wife saves bowling balls, he played at Cedar Rapids." He's reading all that. Now all of a sudden a rainstorm comes and the Red Book and the Green Book get wet. He's dead. He has nothing.

As for Howard, he's all the time telling me that the guy is 29 years old and he went to A & M and he went here and there. That's not telling me anything I couldn't read in a book. I don't call that telling-it-like-it-is. Any man who changes his name and wears a toupee ain't telling-it-like-it-is.

When I comment, I like to have people react in one of two ways: 1) I never thought of it that way; or 2) he doesn't know what he's talking about, here's the way it is.

Brickhouse: Joe, you do a lot of after dinner speeches. Do you have a skeleton format from which you operate? Or do you have speech A, B and C? Or do you fly with it and ad lib a brand new speech each time?

Garagiola: I don't go in with a set speech A, B or C. It's unfair to the people who have asked you there. The first thing I try to do is to make sure I can give the proper time to each speech. I don't think you should go there 10 minutes before and leave two minutes before the last prayer is said.

If you don't want to go, don't go in the first place. A lot of people have worked very hard on these dinners and this is the biggest event of the year for them. That's why I give it my best shot. I try to use local flavor. If I check into a hotel, I talk to the bellboy, the hotel clerk, the guy behind the cigarette counter—and I read all the papers in an effort to get that local angle.

I never work blue. Ballplayers who get up there and start telling dirty stories—that's wrong. It borders on genius stupidity.

If you are not a funny guy, if you don't think funny, you don't have to tell jokes. Some ballplayers are just sincere guys who are glad to sign autographs and answer questions. But to go in there and say, "Oh, I gotta make a speech. Well, I'll tell 'em two Yogi Berra stories, two umpire stories and tell 'em what the catcher says to the pitcher—and then I'll let 'em go for the kind of money they're paying me." That's wrong, that's dead wrong.

You just cannot ad lib a speech. I look at it like catching a ball game. I learn my pitcher's best pitch—and if it's a fastball, I know I got that—and now I look for other pitches. In other words, I write down certain things I know I'm going to say. If nothing else happens in that room, nothing I can play off on, I've still got a good speech so that's my best pitch. I don't have to worry about what I'm going to say when I'm sitting at the head table.

Brickhouse: Joe, how have you handled the pressures of working for a network?

Garagiola: I've tried to handle it by being myself. I can't be anybody else. I'm no more religious than the next guy. But a couple times a week, I go into St. Patrick's. I don't go to Mass and High Mass and all that. A lot of times nobody is there, and I kind of go one-on-one with God. I say. "Look, today's gonna be one of those days and

I'm one of those guys who's liable to get a little ticked, so you're gonna have to help me. Now you've got some saint up there who ain't doin' too much today, so please let him be alongside me."

I know it sounds funny but it works for me. That's my formula. I know what I want. I want to live a normal life. I want my family to have nice things, I want to have nice things. I really am beyond that stage in my life where I gotta have everything, I gotta do everything, and I left the prestigious *Today* show because it was affecting my family life.

I'd feel bad if I went to the ball park and nobody knew who I was—but I don't want that to be the master of me. My friend Jack Paar had the greatest line: "The greatest luxury in the world is to be able to say, 'No, thank you very much.'"

Jack, it's like going to a buffet or a smorgasbord. If your eyes can stay even with your stomach, you're all right, but if your eyes get bigger than your stomach, you're gonna get sick.

Brickhouse: You and Curt Gowdy and Tony Kubek were on hand for NBC when Hank Aaron hit No. 715. What went through your mind?

Garagiola: What made it exciting to me was the way Hank handled the pressure, the build-up. He is a common man and I say that with the greatest respect. He was placed in a great situation and he did things in a way which proved his greatness. He always impressed me as a guy who happened to be walking by home plate and said, "I might as well grab a bat and hit a home run."

He showed humility and something else you see in great stars—inner arrogance. Pete Reiser was the first one I ever heard use that term. It's where you know inside your heart that you're really good, you know you can do it. It's inner confidence. Too many people walk around with it on their sleeve and tell you how good they are—but not Aaron. He knew he was good and he handled it all with dignity.

It's a good thing for baseball and broadcasting that one Joe Garagiola didn't take my advice of many years ago!

Since I am often asked for my opinion of other broadcasters, let me survey the national scene before describing the gentlemen I've worked with in Chicago.

Al Michaels — As I write this, Al is beginning to reach his peak and once he gets there he'll stay there indefinitely. He has paid his dues. In the nature of this business, all successful people have paid their dues. There are no overnight sensations.

Don Meredith — Don and I go back to the days when George Halas drafted him first and then gave him to Dallas in the interests of helping the National Football League. He was a fine quarterback with a fine football mind.

In the booth, I think he had trouble sometimes deciding whether he wanted to be a football expert or a comedian. Consequently, sometimes he was neither. Someday he'll decide what he wants to be and I'm sure he'll be great once he concentrates on one direction.

Frank Gifford — One of the real surprises to me. He is an ex-athlete who knows how to do play-by-play and does a super job. He's a different breed of cat. The play-by-play man has to have a solid vocabulary and has to speak rapidly and be understood and tell the story. You may have all the knowledge in the world about the sport but if you can't speak clearly and rapidly you can't do play-by-play.

I guess I can forgive him now for the great plays he made in the 1956 championship game to help lead the Giants over the Bears, 47-7.

Dick Enberg — Here is another fellow whose work pleases me very much. He's one of the best-educated broadcasters ever and holds a doctorate. But Dick never flaunts his education. He has the common touch and handles situations with dignity. He is one of the very best.

Vin Scully — Here again, I am prejudiced. I've worked alongside Vin assorted times over the years and have been in his company socially. Is there a greater baseball announcer on the scene today? He has that marvelous Irish wit, that beautiful command of the King's English and the great instinct of knowing when to speak and when to shut up.

Curt Gowdy — I can remember Curt so well when he was a young announcer in Wyoming and Oklahoma. He was a good man and a good athlete out west and then he landed a job in Boston and also helped Mel Allen with the Yankees. What impressed me and still does is his ability to handle success and always to be a down-to-earth guy. At no time did he ever turn his head and let his success get the better of him. I consider him a good friend.

Jim McKay — A pro's pro. If I ever owned a network I'd want Jim McKay to work for me. I know two things: He would never do anything but a good broadcast and he'd range from good to outstanding. His versatility is unmatched. He has a working knowledge of sports more so than anyone on the scene. He's worked them all. His job at Munich during the 1972 Olympic Games ranks with the all-time best performances and is a genuine historic moment that will live in broadcasting for the ages. The real pro came out in him that evening when word came that the Israelis had been killed.

Brent Musburger — A genuine surprise to me. I knew Brent when he was a baseball beat man for the Hearst paper in Chicago—Chicago's *American*. We travelled together and later he became a columnist. Then he started working at CBS on the side. I still didn't visualize him as a top broadcaster. Soon thereafter he went to work full time at WBBM radio—the CBS affiliate. The next thing you know he took off. He gets all the credit in the world because I don't think he had the God-given talent to do what he's doing. I don't believe he was given a play-by-play man's voice or great power with the language. I just didn't see him as that type of person. But through shrewd, dogged determination—including the shedding of a lot of weight—coupled with all the extra time and work you can imagine, he made himself into a top-flight broadcaster. To me it's a joy to tune him in and I'm proud that he has succeeded.

Bob Costas — One of the youngsters. I've been around him long enough and I've caught enough of his work to be tremendously impressed. I find that his mind works very fast. He has a good command of the language and his flow is excellent. He also has the talent of letting the event do the explaining. It's not Costas using the event to show off Costas. He will be around for a long, long successful career.

Ted Husing — He was perhaps the perfect announcer — and not simply a sportscaster. While I was starting in Peoria, Husing was the star at CBS radio.

I will never forget the end of the 1935 Ohio State-Notre Dame game with Ted doing the play-by-play. The game was one of the most exciting in NCAA history with Notre Dame coming back in the final moments with two touchdowns. Husing's description of the finish is absolute must listening for any aspiring broadcast student. Ted had everything you could ask from a broadcaster. He had voice, diction, discipline, ego or self-confidence and the ability to work very, very hard. He combined them all.

Lindsey Nelson — I've known Lindsey for 30 years or more. When I was inducted into the National Sports Broadcasters and Sports Writers Hall of Fame, I asked Lindsey to make the presentation. To know Lindsey Nelson and call him a friend is an honor.

Tony Kubek — Every time I listen to Tony I realize I am hearing a genuine baseball authority. He ranks with the best analysts in our field. He has made the transition to the broadcast booth with the same smoothness that characterized his career as a star infielder.

It suddenly occurs to me that I could go on and on and on mentioning quality people at the national level. Russ Hodges. Jack Drees. Joe Boland. Ray Scott. Jack Buck. Chuck Thompson. Ernie Harwell. Pat Summerall. John Madden. Merlin Olson. Ralph Kiner. Bob Uecker. Even though this is a very select list, there are still some names I should have included and I hereby apologize for any omissions.

Now I'd like to say something about my Chicago colleagues over the years. A broadcast booth is a pressure cooker. There are periods when you spend more time in the broadcast booth than you do at home. And there are some days when you go into that booth with a chip on your shoulder or when you're just not feeling right.

Well, anyone who does it for a living had better be prepared to go at least 60 percent of the way with your colleagues every single day. And no one should ever go into that booth without taking his sense of humor with him. It's important to remember that the other guy in there is not only your broadcast partner, he's also your friend and he may not be feeling so well that day.

The guys I've worked with I consider to be among the best friends I've ever had.

There was Harry Creighton, for example. He's the executor of my will and was the childhood guardian of my daughter. Does that express how I feel about Harry Creighton?

Harry also did the greatest job of putting Hamm's beer on the market of anybody except maybe the brewery itself. We took Hamm's from 118 outlets in Cook County to 9,600. I credit Harry with a lot of that. We also worked a lot of football games together.

And there was Marty Hogan, a totally delightful Chicago Irishman who freely admitted that sports announcing was not his bag. Marty primarily was a salesman. He said: "I'm not a sports announcer—I'm a peddler. I sell." He got a brief turn at working baseball with me simply because he brought in sponsors—and I have to say even today it was one of the real fun seasons I ever had.

If he had lived, Jack Quinlan, in my opinion, quite possibly would have established himself as the best sports announcer ever. He had it all: talent, knowledge, personality, perseverance, looks.

Even now, I shudder as I think of that fateful March night in 1965.

Quinlan had left for spring training a few days before me. "Tell you what," I told him prior to his departure, "call me Friday night and we'll set up a golf date."

That Friday night, I had just checked into the Arizona Biltmore in Phoenix when the phone rang. The voice of an elderly man said: "Jack Quinlan has been killed in an automobile accident."

Jack Quinlan was a master at imitating voices, and I was positive this had to be one of his gags. Quinlan couldn't be dead. He was about as alive as any man I ever had known.

The rest is history. Quinlan had played golf that day. En route to his hotel afterwards, his car had skidded on a dangerous curve on Mesa's outskirts and piled into a truck. He was alone. There wasn't much left of him.

Identification of the body was made by Jim Enright of *Chicago Today* and Don Biebel, the Cubs' publicity man. Frankly, I didn't have enough nerve to be there.

We later started a Jack Quinlan Memorial Golf Tournament in his honor. Jack Rosenberg wrote the eulogy for the banquet program. That eulogy has been reprinted in the program at each subsequent tournament. I quote it herewith:

Jack Quinlan and WGN formed an unforgettable parlay. Quinlan had the big sound, the sound which has brought the station greatness. His voice possessed the firmness of a hearty handshake. The resonance of a finely-tuned harp. The clarity of a starry night. The quality of a prayer.

When Quinlan joined WGN in 1958, he filled out a portion of a routine questionnaire in this fashion:

Question: How did you happen to enter radio?

Answer: Always wanted to broadcast sports since childhood.

Question: Approximately how many times have you been on the air?

Answer: Thousands.

Question: What is your greatest extravagance?

Answer: Buying toys for my youngsters.

Those questions, and those answers, give

a brief insight into the life of Jack Quinlan. Unanswered is the question as to why the good die young. Jack was only 38 when he was killed in an auto-truck accident near Cubs' spring training headquarters at Mesa, Arizona, on March 19, 1965.

It is significant that Jack Quinlan became acknowledged as the Radio Voice of the Chicago Cubs. As a youngster—long before his days at New Trier, at Western Military Academy and at Notre Dame—and even longer before his days at WDZ (Tuscola), WMBD (Peoria), WIND and WGN—he sat in the grandstands at Wrigley Field and practiced the play-by-play that was to lift him to the pinnacle of his profession.

The Cubs and the Fighting Irish of Notre Dame—they were Quinlan's first loves, a passionate affair which brought extreme jubilation when they won, utter despair when they lost. Jack Quinlan lived for his family and his faith. He lived for a home run by Banks, a quarterback sneak by Lujack, a no-hitter by Cardwell, an interception by Petitbon, a 40-yard run by Lattner, a miraculous stop by Santo, a 3,000th hit by Musial, an off-tackle smash by Hornung. He lived for the barbecue on the patio, for the sports section on the ride to South Bend, for the after-dinner speech, for the imitation of Lawrence Welk.

It was Rudyard Kipling who said it this way:

"When Earth's last picture is painted, and the tubes are twisted and dried,

When the oldest colors have faded, and
the youngest critic has died,
We shall rest, and faith, we shall need
it—lie down for an aeon or two,
Till the Master of All Good Workmen
shall put us to work anew."

If, in fact, The Master of All Good Workmen has created a play-by-play job in the
Great Beyond, those who have known Jack
Quinlan are positive he is the man behind the
microphone.

Then there's Vince Lloyd. He is one of my
favorite people. We both worked in Peoria. When
I was working in Peoria, Bob Elson helped Jack
Brickhouse get to Chicago. When I got to Chicago
I helped Vince get the introduction he needed to
show what he could do. I just helped get him the
interview. He got himself the job.

When Jack Quinlan died, Vince had the option to take the number one job on the radio or
to remain in the television booth with me. He
opted to be the number one man on radio and it
was certainly a good move for Vince since I stayed
around many more years doing television.

Lloyd Pettit came next. In my opinion he was
one of the most gifted play-by-play men I have
ever known. He was a golden boy athlete at
Northwestern University. There wasn't anything
he couldn't do well.

He did baseball, football and, of course,
hockey. As far as hockey was concerned he was
in a class by himself. Nobody has ever done it better than Lloyd.

Jim West and I worked together for six years and I never had a more pleasurable six years in my life. He was also an outstanding studio announcer. To me that's the test.

What we wanted when we hired Jim was a man who would handle hockey and help out on baseball. He was perfect. Those were six great years.

Then we had a belt-tightening. It was decided that I would work alone for a couple of seasons and that Vince and Lou Boudreau would handle the radio.

Boudreau was the first former athlete to make it big in our broadcasting set-up. I had always felt that an athlete could add to a broadcast and I was right. Lou has fit in perfectly.

I still remember the audition in which Boudreau clinched the job with our management team. We took him into a radio studio and posed a number of hypothetical baseball situations. Lou was told to do an analysis. He took to it as a duck takes to water and the job was his. That was in 1958. In 1960, the Cubs went into an early tailspin. Boudreau agreed to switch places with manager Charlie Grimm. Lou moved to the dugout, Charlie came upstairs to the broadcast booth. When the season ended, Boudreau resumed his announcing chores and the Cubs switched to a "college of coaches" instead of a regular manager in 1961.

I feel there always will be room for the ex-athlete turned broadcaster. And if the play-by-play man is smart, he'll play that color man like a harp to take full advantage of the man's playing experiences.

I met with the WGN people in 1979 and told them, "Look, it's a wonderful company and I've enjoyed a rewarding career. But sooner or later you're going to have to find somebody to replace me."

I threw a couple of names at them and they picked Milo Hamilton, effective in 1980. It was understood that Milo would come in and sit beside me for a couple of years and then he'd take over. He was a great partner. A guy who did his homework. Men like Milo and Philadelphia's By Saam put men like me to shame with their ability to prepare and do their homework.

Then the sands shifted as they sometimes do in our business. Harry Caray became available. Jim Dowdle, the president of Tribune Broadcasting Company, told me he was going to hire Harry. We both understood that he had to straighten it out with Milo. Milo could never quite adjust to it. He wound up taking the Astros' announcing job in Houston in 1985.

Harry and I competed in a friendly sort of way when he was with the White Sox and I was with the Cubs. I remember when he was negotiating his contract with the White Sox. I called and told him I rarely relished the kind of tough competition he offered, but I felt this town would be big enough for both of us.

I am sure Harry got mail about me and I know I got mail about Harry. The typical "Why can't you be more like him" and vice versa. Everyone is going to get that type of mail. It never bothered me. Wouldn't it be boring if everyone sounded the same? Harry has done a spectacular job in Chicago.

In all the years and through all the partners, I have had only one bad experience. That came in 1946 when I was in New York broadcasting the New York Giants' games.

I had been in Chicago before that, but when the war ended and Bob Elson returned from the service, I was bumped from the White Sox job. I understood that. There weren't any hard feelings.

That left me free. I interviewed for the number two position to Mel Allen with the Yankees and was beaten out by Russ Hodges.

I also interviewed for the number one job with the Giants and beat out 100 guys in getting it. The only unpleasant experience I ever had was with my partner that year, Steve Ellis.

I was hired by the Giants and sponsored by Pabst beer, thanks to their advertising director, Nate Perlstein. Steve Ellis was clouted into the job because he was with the station. Ellis hadn't done as much as one inning of baseball his entire life— not even Little League. I told him it was nothing personal, but I was opposed to him getting the job. I told him that this was my life and my career and he hadn't even done an inning.

But anyway, here we were together; a team in the broadcast booth doing games for a bad baseball team. When you're covering a bad baseball team, you, the announcers, take as much heat as the club itself. I know because I did my share of bad baseball clubs. On the other side, when the team is winning, everything you say is great.

I told Ellis, "You will listen and I will teach you. I hope we will both gain from this experience and that we'll become good friends." He professed amazement at my honesty.

He used so many cliches and slang expressions that tears came to my eyes. Cliches and slang are like salt and pepper, a little here and there adds seasoning to the game. But too much destroys the broadcast.

Well, he had a press agent in New York. One day I picked up Walter Winchell's column in New York and what do I see but one line that says, "Steve Ellis hits a home run as the Giants' broadcaster."

The final story is this: I didn't take the Giants job the next year. It was decided that Frankie Frisch would take over for Ellis.

When I went in for my contract talks they told me that they had to go a little higher than they expected to get Frisch to take the job. I said, "Frankie Frisch is one of my heroes and he should get all he can. He's going to get all the press, the exposure and everything else which he richly deserves. But when that light goes on and the broadcast begins it'll be me that carries Frisch through the games." I told them I thought I should get paid for it.

I asked them to put me on a 10-minute show so we could make up the difference. They said they couldn't do that because Steve Ellis was already hired for that.

I decided to take a pass and returned to Chicago. I enjoyed the New York experience very much. But that wasn't one of the things I cherished.

Steve Ellis and I turned out to be friends. Later on, he did a double take when he realized it could have been a great year for both of us. He told me he wished he had it to do over again. He admitted he hadn't given me the benefit of his cooperation.

I came back to Chicago in 1947. It was then that television began to gain in popularity.

Soon afterward, Navy captain Bill Eddy started me in television. Eddy and I had some conversations and one thing led to another. We went to lunch one day and Eddy said he was thinking about me doing his baseball games on WBKB television. He also said I'd be working with Joe Wilson, one of the finest guys I have ever known.

I took it. I didn't do it for the money. I was doing fine in radio. But I wanted to get into this television thing and find out what it was all about.

We decided to do it with Joe and me splitting $70 per game. Bill Eddy and I went to lunch to put the finishing touches on our deal. Remember, I was going to receive $35 a game for 77 games. Somehow, we had that extra drink at lunch and we got into an argument about who was the better table tennis player. We decided to go over to Bensinger's on Randolph Street and play a best of three. The stakes were double or nothing for the whole season's pay. Eddy said, "We'll go back to my office in the State-Lake Building first because I have to make a couple of phone calls."

I waited a long time outside his office and he never came out. Then it dawned on me. If I beat him he'd have to pay double and even though it was comparative peanuts, he still had a budget. And if he beat me, he'd eventually have unhappy talent working for him and there's no percentage in that. I'm glad we both sobered up.

I worked with Joe and everything was great.

He also got off one of the great one-liners I've heard.

The National Anthem was played by two college bands one day. Both played it in a different key, producing an ear-splitting horror. When it was over, Joe said, "You've just heard the National Anthem played as Salvador Dali would have painted it."

If I started out today with what I started out with in 1934, I doubt if I could get by any good receptionist. I didn't have a lot to offer.

Radio was in its infancy.

Television was still a gleam in someone's eye.

In those days, radio didn't even know in what direction it was headed. It was a baby itself. It was a time when you could make a lot of mistakes and still keep your job.

Today, even the smaller stations demand a finished product. While opportunities are important, there is more to making it in the field of broadcasting than just opportunities.

If I were giving advice to young people today on becoming a broadcaster, I'd say first off be a broadcaster—not a specialist.

In other words, don't say "I want to be a sportscaster" or "I want to be a newscaster" and then put on blinders. You don't do that if you are training to be a doctor or a lawyer. First, you get that basic education—then you specialize.

When I started out, a college education in broadcasting wasn't that important. And I'd say there was a time when it wasn't important because of inexperienced faculties.

For many years the teachers were really only reading one chapter ahead of their students. They never really had gone out into the street and tried to make a living at the business. Today, I'm happy to say almost every college that has a broadcasting school has a good one.

Consequently, when you go for a job be prepared to do as many things as possible. Especially in that first position. That is the time to probe and find out where your talent is. It is important to find your strengths and weaknesses. After a while you may discover you'd be better suited as a director or a producer or a writer or advertising salesman. I can list many people who became interested in the broadcasting end of the field, then were successful in another segment of the industry. They found where their real talent was and they finally had that little talk with themselves and changed course.

Examples: Jack Jacobson started out as a cameraman, then became a great sports director and later a television programming executive. Arne Harris originally wanted to be a sports announcer but was to find that his great strength lay in TV sports directing. Today, he's at the top of the heap in his end of the business. Bill Lotzer moved from a crack career in the sports director's chair to become production chief at WGN Television. All three of these outstanding directors were backed up by what I consider the finest technical crew in the history of the industry . . . . the WGN Television crew.

Once you discover what your strengths and weaknesses are and you find the right position, then you concentrate on that area. You work 28 hours a day, eight days a week. There is no such thing as a part-time broadcaster. I don't know how many times I've been approached by somebody who has a good job but wants to do some broadcasting on the side. It seldom works.

That's because the people who become successful dedicate themselves to it. By nature I am a lazy guy unless I'm doing something I love. I fell in love with the broadcasting business.

When I first started in Peoria in 1934, if you worked an 80-hour week you were still dogging it. I worked late and I worked long.

I also listened all the time to my elders. I enjoyed their company.

As I look back, there weren't too many successful people who didn't ask a lot of questions of people who had been there.

You can't put a price tag on that type of experience and you can't explain it unless you've been through it.

The competition is heavy. There are thousands of men and women who are willing to devote their lives full-time to a career in broadcasting. If they are going against people who only want to do it part-time, the part-timers don't have a chance.

Broadcasting is a great career, a great business and it's getting better all the time.

V

"Bear Down, Bears"

August, 1985. The Ritz-Carlton. WGN Television's fall premier, a fancy bash put on by the sales department. The emcee is Tom Dreesen, comedian. And a real good one. He introduces the Cubs' players and other sports dignitaries, then focuses on me.

"Ladies and gentlemen," he says, "here's Hall of Famer Jack Brickhouse." The usual applause. Then Dreesen adds: "Do you realize that tens of thousands of people grew up not knowing anything about football because they listened to Jack Brickhouse and Irv Kupcinet on the Bears' broadcasts? Right, Kup? That's right, Jack."

Everyone laughed, including me. And they can laugh all they want.

The bottom line is that Kup and I broadcast the Bears for 24 straight seasons. How many comedians have shows that run that long?

Our broadcasts were sold out every year. Thank you, Standard Oil. Thank you, G. Heileman Brewing Company. Thank you, many others.

Our broadcasts enjoyed immense ratings.

And we were imitated far and wide, which supposedly is a form of flattery.

Kup to me was an ideal partner for Bears' football. He had played the game in college and later, briefly, as a pro. He had officiated in the NFL. And he gave the broadcasts a certain celebrity status because of the guests he attracted at halftime.

I'll never forget the day the half had just ended when Harry Truman, Bob Hope and newly-crowned middleweight champ Carmen Basilio walked into the booth looking for Kup.

Those were the days.

It's funny which events stand out in my memory from the hundreds of Bears' games I covered. Let me relate one which I think illustrates the human side of sports.

It is December 14, 1974, and I am en route to O'Hare to meet Jack Rosenberg. It seems now I have spent half my life going to O'Hare to meet Rosey. Or Arne Harris. Or Jack Jacobson. Or Bill Lotzer. Or Vince Lloyd. Or Lou Boudreau. Or Jim West. Or Lloyd Pettit. Or Irv Kupcinet. Sometimes our WGN crews travel together, sometimes not. Sometimes we take team charters, sometimes not.

But whatever, it's a syndrome. We're always going or coming.

Sports is a great common denominator. The cabbie knows why I am going to O'Hare. The skycap knows why I am there. So does the man behind the counter for the airlines. They invariably know where the Cubs, White Sox or Bears are playing next and they offer a pertinent comment. I am recognized by many at O'Hare and it is flattering, just as it is humbling when I arrive at the other end and find people who don't know me from Adam.

On this particular December day, I am booked on Flight #116, American Airlines, Chicago O'Hare to Washington's National Airport in the nation's capital. I am fidgety. I know I am about to cover Abe Gibron's last game as head coach of the Chicago Bears. He is matched against the Redskins on Sunday and the outcome is immaterial. Abe is gone and I have been sure of it since mid-November. No one really has to make an official announcement.

I detest situations of this type. A broadcaster develops certain ties. I have found Abe Gibron to be a sincere and dedicated family man. His sin is that as boss of the Bears he simply didn't win enough. It is a plague common to the coaching profession.

I check the big board at O'Hare. Flight #116 goes from Gate K-11. Why do I always leave from K-ll? Or H-12? The far gates. And at my age. Yet, my family doctor tells me I should walk more — and I tell him to follow me around O'Hare for a month. At any rate, O'Hare has a festive look. The decorations. Passengers with holiday bundles. I head past the newspaper stand and gift shop. I used to be curious about the toys there, but Jeanne had grown up now. I go to the area marked "Entrance to Gates — Passengers & Visitors." The security check is routine.

The path to K-ll is lined with billboards. O'Hare International Tower Hotel. LaPreferida Foods. Continental Bank. Dunhill International Cigarettes. Robert L. Nelson Real Estate, Inc. Wool

Bureau, Inc. Hyatt Hotels. The Wall Street Journal. Budget Rent a Car. So on down the line.

An airline pilot who has just completed a flight from Los Angeles stops me and tells of his collection of baseball memorabilia. He is excited because Mickey Mantle was on a recent trip and gave him an autographed picture. He wants to know if the Bears have a chance at Washington and I don't have the heart to tell him my true feelings.

The flight to Washington is uneventful. I lose three dollars to Rosey playing gin. So what else is new?

The cabbie at National Airport notices the personalized bag tags on our luggage. He says: "You guys must be here for the game. I can tell you right now I don't care for that 'win at all costs' theory of George Allen." The cab turns for the Crystal City Marriott in Arlington, Virginia. All along, I am wondering whether George Allen's theory is different from that of any other football coach.

As we reach the Marriott, the cabbie muses: "I saw the Bears beat Washington, 73-0, in 1940. You know, Sammy Baugh threw a sure touchdown pass for the Redskins early in that game but it was dropped. They asked him afterwards if it would have made any difference and he said: 'Yes, the final score would have been 73-7.' " The cabbie is pleased at his recollection and our reaction to it.

I call Gibron. Maybe we can all have dinner together. He invites us to his suite. He is watching a television special: "Portrait: Legend in Granite." It is the story of Vince Lombardi. I watch Abe's face. It is stoic even as Lombardi, portrayed by Ernest Borgnine, hands out fur coats to the Packers' wives in a burst of emotion. Abe's countenance remains impassive as Lombardi fines Max McGee $500 for breaking curfew and threatens him with $1,000 the next time. Lombardi says something like: "If you find a gal worth $1,000, call me, too. I'd like to see her myself." Still no reaction from Abe.

I know that Abe knows at this moment that he has had it with the Bears.

I think that Abe is thinking at this moment what might have been, how maybe if the Fates had smiled kindly perhaps he, Abe Gibron, could have been another Lombardi. Or another Paul Brown. After all, Abe learned his lessons from Brown as a player at Cleveland.

The show ends; we watch the Oakland-Dallas game briefly on the tube and then, with the Cowboys in front, 7-3, we take off for the Rotunda, a fashionable Washington restaurant. Abe goes with a group of Washington friends in one car, we follow behind in a cab with a Bears' defensive coach, Chuck Cherundolo. He is a loyal man. He says: "If only they would give Abe one more turn, one more year. I know he could turn it around. He deserves another chance."

At the restaurant, Abe's popularity is evident. He was an assistant coach with the Redskins at one time and, on this night, people from various walks of life greet him with handshakes and embraces that have to touch his inner being.

Abe pauses at dinner. "You know," he says, "this whole thing is tough on my kids. I'm always going to find a job, I'm not worried about that. But my kids take a lot of heat from other kids at school. That's what bothers me."

It is game day now. Kup, Rosey and I make the trek skyward to the visitors radio booth in the upper strata of Robert F. Kennedy Stadium. How I avoid a nosebleed at that elevation is beyond me. Only Municipal Stadium in Cleveland can rival RFK Stadium for lousy broadcasting conditions at big-time sports events.

A banner stretched across the upper deck facade opposite us proclaims: "Like A Fine Wine, Sonny Gets Better With Age." That sign was to become prophetic before the day was out.

Washington wins the toss and receives. The Redskins fail to move the ball and Mike Bragg punts. The Bears take over on their own 33. The offense, lethargic all season, with one streak of 22 scoreless quarters to prove it, startles the Redskins on first down. Quarterback Bobby Douglass un-corks a bomb. Bo Rather races behind the defense at the Washington nine. Douglass lays the ball in his hands. Rather drops it, then stretches out on the turf for a moment in disbelief.

The game is seconds old and already the tide has turned, perhaps the story of Gibron's life as head coach of the Bears.

Washington's 40-year-old quarterback, Sonny Jurgensen, takes it from there. His passing sets up two second quarter touchdown runs by Larry Brown. He hits Charley Taylor from 11 yards out for a third score. It is 21-0 at halftime and the only question is the final margin. Yes, Jurgensen, like a fine wine, gets better with age.

I sneak occasional looks at the coaches, Allen and Gibron, as the score mounts. The contrast is staggering.

On the Washington side, there is George Allen, the ice cream man. They call him that because of his fondness for ice cream, but in a manner of speaking, he deserves the monicker if for no other reason than the fact he has a cool and refreshing look.

As I glance at Allen, I can't help but recall his brilliant work as defensive coach of the Bears in 1963. The players voted him the game ball after the Bears stopped the New York Giants, 14-10, to capture the world championship.

A few seasons later, Allen had been hauled into court by George Halas, Sr., in a contract dispute. Allen lost, but once Halas had proved his point, he allowed Allen to get out of his contract and go to the Los Angeles Rams as head coach.

Allen moved on to Washington in 1971 and signed a fantastic contract. The Redskins' president, Edward Bennett Williams, was to say: "I gave George Allen an unlimited budget and he already has exceeded it."

The week before the Bears' game, I had read an item in the *Los Angeles Times* quoting Allen thusly: "I don't send Christmas cards. How do Christmas cards help you win? It makes more sense just to tell your friends Merry Christmas. I can use the money to buy another projector."

That's a quotable line, especially when you're winning, and on this particular day in December of 1974, George Allen looks the part of a winner. He gives it the Joe College approach. He has a gleeful way of rubbing his hands, of clapping, of licking his fingers as if preparing to count a stack of certificates of deposit.

He shakes hands repeatedly with his players as they trot on and off. Len Hauss. Rusty Tillman. Brig Owens. Chris Hanburger. Most of the rest. The band dutifully plays "Hail to the Redskins" following each touchdown and you get the feeling George Allen regards it as a second national anthem.

Here he is, the author of six books, and only an hour or so earlier a young fellow who is a friend of *Chicago Daily News* writer Tim Weigel has told me he was reading Allen's *The Future Is Now* in the wee hours of this very day while awaiting delivery of a baby daughter.

On the Bears' side, there is Abe Gibron, hands in pockets, forlorn, oblivious to the biting winds. Then it's 28-0, then 35-0, then 42-0. The winners tell jokes, the losers yell deal. And here is Gibron, despite the bitterness of defeat, telling reporters after the game: "I've never quit, and I never will. I could walk out and put the blame on a lot of people, but I'm not built that way. I can only say that I pick the Redskins to go all the way now. They've got the momentum."

A long weekend for all concerned. I have seen once again the peaks and valleys of coaching. I arrive home and get a call from WGN. Ara Parseghian, the coach of defending national champion Notre Dame, has resigned. "I've been exhausted for two years," Parseghian's statement says. "The pressure is terrific."

You go figure it.

I've broadcast Bears-Packers games since the Year One and only one thing has remained constant: I never have gotten a good night's sleep in Green Bay the night before the showdown.

Bears' fans traditionally move into Packerland in big numbers, no matter the team records. They sing and dance and whoop it up. I get the feeling that any Bears' booster who has spent the weekend in Green Bay and still finds himself able to go to work on Monday simply hasn't given his all.

On this particular Saturday night, I had gone to dinner down the street from the Northland Hotel, then returned to my room to check over the depth charts. I knew the numbers of Starr and Taylor and Hornung and Nitschke like I knew my own telephone number. That's no big deal. Most schoolboys in the Illinois-Wisconsin area knew them, too.

But a handful of new players show up in every pro game, so you find yourself checking numbers until kickoff. A veteran announcer once jokingly told me he prepared for a game by learning the numbers of the backs and ends during the taxi ride en route to the stadium, then he would throw in the names of the interior linemen during the broadcast in case their mothers were listening.

In any event, I turned off the lights at midnight and fell asleep.

At 2 A.M. came that unmistakable sound. Loud voices obviously fortified by beer.

"Bear down, Chicago Bears," they sang, lustily and off-key, to the accompaniment of a booming bass drum and a blaring trumpet. Up and down the halls of the second floor they marched, reaching a crescendo when the lyrics carried them to the part about "pride and joy of Illinois, Chicago Bears, bear down!"

Finally, I stuck my head out the door to confront the Chicago Bears Fan Tour face-to-face. "Listen, fellows," I said, "how about toning it down just a little. I have to work today."

From the end of the hall, an inebriate screamed: "Hey, ain't you Brickhouse?"

"I am, as a matter of fact," I answered.

"Brickhouse is a jackass," he yelled. "Hey heyyyyy."

You could hear him all over the place, the word "jackass" piercing the atmosphere, and it brought the house down. One by one, I saw doors opening and faces emerging to laugh their tails off at my predicament.

The troubadours insisted I join them for a drink. There was no turning back. A half-hour later, I was singing "Bear down, Chicago Bears," too. It occurred to me that if the Bears' team had this exuberance, they would beat the seven-point spread.

No such luck.

Quite often over the years, the Bears and Packers have battled for football supremacy in the snow. It was on such a day at Wrigley Field that a Green Bay rooter approximating 300 pounds, properly fortified by the contents of his flask, held his Packer banner high and bravely paraded back and forth in front of the solid Bears' rooting section.

He was pelted by dozens of snowballs but continued undaunted until he had made the rounds.

Of such stuff are champions made.

Still another year and another game at Green Bay brought an unforgettable incident that tickled George Halas.

A grizzled Packer Backer stood on the walk outside the Northland at 4 A.M. on Sunday, lifted a bullhorn to his lips and blared: "Halas, if you're half a man, you'll come down and fight!"

As sure as there is a human side of sports, there is a humorous one as well. Paul Hornung was a fabulous runner on Vince Lombardi's wondrous Green Bay teams of the 1960s. Some years after Miami had won two straight Super Bowls, and finished one season unbeaten, I asked Hornung how the Packers of his era would have fared against the Dolphins.

Said Hornung with a grin: "I've already inquired and we would be favored over Miami by anywhere from 7 to 10 points!"

I also learned to tread lightly when taking on a moose.

George (Moose) Connor weighed two pounds at birth, then grew up to become a football immortal at Notre Dame and with the Bears. The audience included Vice-President Gerald Ford the night Moose laid it on me at a Frank Leahy Memorial dinner in Oakbrook.

"I was a rookie with the Bears in '48," Connor grinned, "and Coach Halas needed a kicker. That was the season before George Blanda showed up in camp. I had handled the kick-offs at Notre Dame and now Halas wanted me to to go in and try my first field goal.

"It was an exciting moment for me. I figured

this was my chance to become another Lou Groza. Bulldog Turner, our center, snapped the ball, little J. R. Boone put it down, and I moved toward it with my size 15 shoe. I swung my leg mightily — took out a big divot — and kicked a low line drive which hit Bulldog Turner right in the hind end. And up in the broadcast booth I understand Jack Brickhouse hollered, 'Watch it now — the Bears got a trick play. Hey hey . . . .' "

I don't remember saying that, but Moose got a big laugh and I can't knock success!

Moose and I both laughed at a story Henry Jordan of the Packers told at another football banquet. It concerned the Packers' Super Bowl game against the Kansas City Chiefs.

The way Jordan told it, Chiefs' owner Lamar Hunt entered his team's dressing room before the game and said: "If you men beat the Packers, I'll double the jackpot."

When the word of that offer filtered over to Green Bay's coach, Vince Lombardi, he told the Packers: "If you men beat the Chiefs, you can call me by my first name!"

You all remember who won.

I've been a party to my share of sports history but never had I heard the Bears' fight song played or sung in late January until 1986. There simply had been no reason to play or sing it at that time of the year.

The Bears changed all that on January 26, 1986, by crushing the New England Patriots, 46-10, to win their first Super Bowl. They did it in the

70-degree warmth of the Louisiana Superdome and I couldn't help but harken back to that 11-degree day of December 29, 1963, when the Bears beat the New York Giants, 14-10, to grab the NFL title in pre-Super Bowl days.

And I got the feeling that somewhere up there George Halas was smiling as his grandson, Bears' president Michael McCaskey, raised the Super Bowl trophy ironically named in honor of Vince Lombardi, Halas' friendly adversary of a bygone era.

Mike Ditka was one of my favorites as a hard-nosed Bears' tight end, so it was particularly pleasing to me to watch him coach what quite possibly was the best football team ever.

I was broadcasting the Bears when Ditka got $5,899 as his share of the '63 championship money. He probably would like to be around if they ever have a Super Bowl where each winning player gets $100,000 and each losing player gets nothing.

But don't ask me to referee it.

VI

Owners and Other Brass

Since I was a rookie, the world has changed. The world survived a second World War, the battlefields of Korea and Vietnam, and countless other tragedies as well as historical achievements that would absolutely amaze our ancestors.

One of the many changes in sports has been in the form of ownership. The family concept has gone the way of running boards and three cent newspapers. The owners in the 1980s are for the most part not solitary figures, but conglomerates. It is not fathers leaving franchises to their sons and daughters as much as it is directorships changing hands.

For many years sports were sports and business was business. Today sports are still sports, but they are a business as well. A very big business.

Make no mistake, one aspect has remained constant. It is still the owners' bat and ball, football and helmet, basketball and backboard.

It wasn't until my last few years of broadcasting baseball that the game's owners began to change. For most of my career I was blessed with the opportunity to deal with individuals whose love for the game, in many ways, surpassed their love for the business.

Today's sports marketplace is filling up with corporate ownership. If sports were in the game of Monopoly, it would be like Marvin Gardens being bought by the Park Places and Boardwalks.

In earlier times, ownership was intimate. I was glad to say I was able to know and to cover some of the finest and most decent people in the business.

No matter what profession, the great leaders all have one common trait. They all have foresight. Chicago sports have been blessed with owners who could see into the future. Many were pillars in their sport.

For instance, George Halas sat in an automobile showroom in Canton, Ohio and helped draw up the plan for the National Football League. Phil Wrigley cautioned his fellow baseball owners about the reserve clause years before free agency was ever mentioned on the sports page. Arthur Wirtz was concerned that some long-term contracts being offered in sports would never be honored and he made sure he could always honor any contract to which he affixed his name. And, of course, Bill Veeck. The man was always two steps ahead of everyone.

When you talk of interesting franchises and owners, you have to include the Chicago Cardinals football team and its owner, Charlie Bidwill. One son, Stormy, is now involved in operating Sportsman's Park and Churchill Downs. Another son, Billy, runs the team which today is the St. Louis football Cardinals.

Charlie Bidwill always dressed in blue and had two main sports projects: the Blue Birds, a girls softball team, and, of course, the Cardinals. Charlie was determined to make the Cardinals a winner and he did just that when he put together what was to become the dream backfield—Charlie Trippi, Pat Harder, Elmer Angsman and Paul Christman. The coach was Jimmy Conzelman.

I remember Charlie as a unique character. He even loaned money once to George Halas to help the Bears. He was that kind of guy.

In the spring of 1947, just when the Cardinals were on the brink of greatness, Charlie died. The man who then took over as Cardinals' president was Ray Bennigsen. He became one of the best executives this city has ever known. Not only did Ray run the franchise with great integrity, he protected the interests of the Bidwill family. He can compare favorably with the sports leaders of any era.

Vi Bidwill, Charlie's widow, later married Walter Wolfner of St. Louis. Wolfner decided he would run the team. I never have seen a franchise mishandled as badly. It was a shame.

To me, George Halas was one of the great people of all-time. He may have been the toughest single person I've ever known from a physical, emotional and business sense.

The agony and pain he experienced before and after hip surgery was staggering. He lost his wife, a woman to whom he was deeply devoted. And he lost his son—the apple of his eye. And he watched as many of his close friends died. Through the sorrow, he pushed onward and he always kept going.

He was very tough. On the other hand, nobody gave, silently, to more charities than Halas. There were a number of players and associates whom he helped and who then turned around and bit him on the tail. He wasn't always a wealthy man. In fact, it wasn't until 1959 that George didn't have to go to the bank to open the season.

For instance, the first year the Bears played their home games at Wrigley Field, Halas had to wait for the first $20 to go into the till on game day so he could take the money and go across the street to buy tape for his players. But he'd help as many people as he could.

His respect for the dollar was well-known and well-documented. We were playing golf one day after he signed Dick Butkus to a $200,000 contract. I said, "George, knowing you that is $1,000 a year for 200 years." He and Butkus had their problems together. Yet when Dick was inducted into the Pro Football Hall of Fame, he asked Halas to present him with the award. And Halas did.

There was a time when I received an award at a function and, I, too, asked Halas to present it to me. I told George never again—it's my moment in the spotlight and who gets three standing ovations—George Halas.

One of the things I liked best about George was what occurred in 1963 when the Bears won the National Football League title. For the previous two years everyone was saying Halas was too old, that the game had passed him by. Then suddenly he coached a team that won it all. He was heralded as one of the great coaching geniuses at 68 years of age. Suddenly, he was tough, canny, wily, shrewd and a genius.

He was a great one. He was definitely a man for his time.

Above all, Halas did things for people.

Although I've broadcast many sports and did more baseball broadcasts than any other sport, my first love as a kid was basketball.

Pro basketball in Chicago took a long time to gain acceptance. There were quite a few owners who tried to start teams only to watch the teams fold soon thereafter.

For example, there was the Chicago Gears. A well-meaning guy named Maurice White owned a gear company and decided to give pro basketball a try in a league that was a forerunner to the National Basketball Association. His star was George Mikan. I was the broadcaster. Before it was over, Mikan tried to get out of his contract and I tried to get the money they owed me.

Besides the gear company, White also owned horses in Missouri. He brought in a man from Missouri to be the Gears' general manager. His name was C. Guy Grimm. He was the only man in sports I knew who could rival Walter Wolfner as the worst franchise operator in Chicago history.

C. Guy Grimm wanted me to do their broadcasts. They had 22 games scheduled and they offered me what was then a fair price of $200 per game. After my conference with Mr. Grimm I thought we had a deal. Now, this same year, the Chicago Stags came into being. They played at the Chicago Stadium. The Stags offered me a chance to do their games. I had to turn them down because I already had a deal with the Gears.

Days passed and there was still no contract. I called him and asked and also inquired what station we were going to be on. He said they hadn't determined it yet, but they were working on it. He continued to keep stalling. Finally, it was the night before the very first game and I still didn't have a contract. He did, however, find a station, WCFL.

I thought that would be fine. It was a good 50,000 watt station with a great dial position.

I said, "Nice going." He said, "Yeah, but there is just one little thing."

I said, "What's that?" He said, "We can only do half the game."

I said, "That's not the way I had hoped it would work out. But on the other hand basketball being the game it is, if we do pick it up in the second half and give a little recap maybe we can still have a good program."

"Well," he said, "unfortunately, the only time slot we can get is the first half."

He said, "That's the way it is. They (the station) are willing to take it, but the only time slot that's available is an hour during the first half."

I said, "You've got to be crazy." He said that was the best deal he could make. I did the first half the next day. After I signed off, the public was so damned incensed, they almost torched the station.

I told C. Guy Grimm this thing was dead. He concurred. I said, "I'll take my pay and I'll be on my way." He said, "If you don't work the games, you can't get paid."

I said, "I've been trying to get a contract out

of you for three months." Next thing you know, Maurice White got back into the act.

Mikan sued to get out of his contract. I contacted a lawyer friend and we also decided to sue. On the night before we went to court, Maurice White settled. I told my lawyer to go back to Maurice White and if he promised to never ever foist C. Guy Grimm on the Chicago sports scene again to insult the intelligence of professional media people, I would even forget about the settlement.

I'll guarantee you that any one of his horses could have handled it better than he did.

Years later came one of the great people I've ever known, Dave Trager. He headed up a group that created the Chicago Packers. It wasn't that bad a ball club. But it couldn't get decent press coverage. Pro basketball just hadn't caught on in Chicago.

I was handling the contracts at WGN and I went to Dave and we talked. We made a deal to do 10 to 12 games at a real low price. Trager was a smart enough guy to know that at least his club would be getting coverage.

Trager's club still just didn't get the press following it needed. Plus the NBA wasn't all that great and finally the other associates started hounding him a little so he sold out to Abe Pollin in Baltimore, who still owns the ball club (the Washington Bullets.)

Later came the franchise put together by Dick Klein—the Chicago Bulls. Dick was with the Packers who later changed names and became the Zephyrs.

Klein revived the franchise by getting an expansion franchise. He put together a pretty good basketball team. He was and is a brilliant basketball mind.

One thing I always liked about Dick was he always kept his word. We were going to make a deal for the Bulls to be on WGN Television. Dick and I went to one of his favorite places, Matty's Wayside Inn in Glenview.

We both knew we had at least two things in common: We both liked to drink stingers. And we both knew that Channel 32 had given the Bulls an offer that was very good on paper. But WGN was still the number one sports station. He knew he needed the exposure more than he needed a little extra money.

On about the fifth or sixth stinger, we agreed and wrote out a six-year deal on a paper placemat. We knew what we were doing. He signed it and that was all it took.

A day or so later, in a meeting with his owners, he told them about this contract and he said he was sticking with it. In the meantime, I took the placemat to WGN and had a Polaroid camera shot taken of it. I then sent it to the sales department and our sales manager, John McDaniels. He said, "Let me get this straight. We're supposed to go out and sell this feature on the basis of this?"

He wanted to call the squad for me right then and there.

But that deal held up for six years and I lived to see 18,000 people in the Chicago Stadium for basketball. I knew that night that pro basketball had finally been accepted in Chicago.

Owners are always "bottom-line" conscious. You can't blame them for that. One of the most "bottom-line" men of all was Arthur Wirtz, who owned the Black Hawks, Bulls and the Chicago Stadium.

The man's main concern was keeping the Chicago Stadium busy. He was a stickler for making certain that the bottom line always came out right, yet he had a certain flair for creativity. He conceived the Sonja Henie tour and the ice shows, among other notable successes.

Whenever anyone talked about the Black Hawks and Wirtz they always brought up the Bobby Hull situation. Hull left the Black Hawks for the Winnipeg club in the new World Hockey Association after he and Wirtz could not reach agreement on a contract.

If they both had it to do over again, I am certain they would have reached an agreement. Arthur would have had to soften a little and so would Bobby.

Bobby Hull belonged with the Black Hawks. His leaving was unfortunate. But it happens when dollars and egos are involved.

Yet while he was known for being dollar conscious Wirtz was also a very giving person. I got into it one time with Arthur over a charity function.

I was the chairman of the Heart Association one year—I lost a daughter to heart disease. I wanted to do a night at the Stadium as a fund-raiser. Wirtz said he only had a certain number of nights he could fill the Stadium and he wanted to know if I could fill it on this night with the function.

Finally, he said that if I passed on using the Stadium he would guarantee a big contribution. I agreed. Months later, the contribution had not been sent. I called a few times and I kept getting vague answers. I figured he had welched on the deal. I said so to a few people.

Finally, Art called for a meeting. Having been occupied with his many projects, he had the impression the contribution had been sent. When he found it hadn't, he took care of it right away. He was the voice of real reason. We became great friends. I came to know Arthur Wirtz as a man who was very generous in many ways.

When Elizabeth Wirtz died, Arthur started to die right then. Anyone who loved his wife that much and was that much a family man couldn't have been that tough. There was a soft side to him.

As an owner, he took the Black Hawks and the Bulls at a time when there wasn't much fiscal integrity or good sense in sports contracts. Arthur was one of the few steadfast owners who tried to control the situation. He felt if contracts were going to be long-term the money should be placed in escrow. I can name a couple of franchises that can't afford to pay their future bills.

There were people who viewed Arthur Wirtz in two different lights. There were those who knew him and had the greatest respect for the man and saw him as one of the truly great people. But the man on the street probably thought Wirtz was too money conscious.

I know the way the media and the press reacted to him at times bothered him. He was a sensitive guy. When Elizabeth died the fight started to leave him.

Whether or not he is ever recognized as such, Arthur Wirtz was one of the giants in sports.

On to baseball.

The Comiskey family.

One of the questions I was asked most while WGN was broadcasting both Cubs and White Sox games was whether I was a Cubs or White Sox fan. I know a lot of people won't believe this, but I had no favorite and the reason is easy to explain.

When I first came to Chicago, I needed all the help I could get and I received it from both sides of town.

I can't say enough about the Comiskey family. First, there was Grace Comiskey, the matriarch of the family. And there was the daughter, Dorothy, who married John Rigney, and Chuck Comiskey, the son. He was a good kid.

When I came on the scene, there was Grace, Harry Grabiner, the general manager, and Jimmy Dykes, the manager. The whole group said to me, "What can we do to help?"

One of the things I have always admired about Grace Comiskey was her strong will. Against the advice of her counselors and her best friends, who told her to sell the club, she had the courage of her convictions.

She refused time and again. It was Comiskey's dream to have his son, Chuck, run the ball club. She fought off the bank and everyone else in trying to see that Charles Comiskey's dream came true.

As things turned out, the greater authority went to Dorothy and it caused a minor rift in the family. But I'll always respect Grace's moxie. She fended off the banks, the financial experts and everyone else with clout. The fact that the White Sox were finally sold was not her fault.

Bill Veeck's group followed. Then Art and John Allyn. Their father had been in business with Veeck.

Through their father, the sons not only had a ball club but also a small dynasty. Both were strong-willed men. For quite a while John, being the younger, sat in the background.

Later, Arthur got a little carried away in his enthusiasm to make the White Sox even more important than they were.

He had seriously thought about moving from Comiskey Park. He thought he had it sold. There was the time he called what he termed "the most important press conference in Chicago sports history."

He unveiled a new very, very big plan for a complex that would house baseball, football and also have an indoor stadium adjacent to the main stadium. The football stadium would have been called Halas Stadium.

The key question we asked was "Where?" He had access to land just north of the Northwestern train station located on Canal Street.

He made one big mistake. He thought he had the land committed—all but say 10 percent. He thought he had everything in hand. Well, he couldn't get it together.

The most important press conference in Chicago sports history turned out to be not quite that important.

Meanwhile, personnel moves on the ball club weren't sitting too well with John. So, John and Art put their heads together and both agreed they couldn't make it without cutting up the empire. John kept the ball club.

One other thing Art had done turned out to be a serious mistake for the White Sox. That was not renewing their contract with WGN-TV.

They had a very good deal with WGN-TV. We did both White Sox and Cubs' home games.

Ed Short, who was the general manager, and I sat down and did the preliminary negotiating. We thought we had the deal worked out. At that point we brought it back to our superiors.

Ed Short and I put the finishing touches on the deal.

Next thing we knew, a luncheon was called. Art Allyn showed up and said he was not going back with WGN-TV. He said the White Sox were going to WFLD—Channel 32.

The Channel 32 offer on paper was very good. Their boss, Red Quinlan, put it together and it was a good move on his part.

Chicago was a VHF town, which meant the television channels were between 2 and 13. Well, Channel 32 was UHF and Quinlan knew he had to get something exclusive on his station to get people to buy the UHF sets or have their sets adapted to receive the signal on Channel 32.

WFLD and the White Sox signed a five-year deal with an option for five more.

Arthur dropped that bomb on us and sent us to the Cubs exclusively.

The big mistake was not realizing what they needed most of all was exposure, not money.

Consequently, their audiences dropped off. It became even more important because the ball club wasn't winning.

Later, when John owned the team, he even had trouble getting a radio outlet for a while and he was having a tough time making their ball club better. All in all, everything didn't work out as well as expected. The White Sox had fallen on evil times.

At that point, there was talk and a threat of the club moving.

Many of us decided we weren't going to let the franchise, whose original owner founded the American League, leave town.

John was determined to keep it in Chicago. I got a group together and for the second time Bill Veeck put a group together. Veeck made the buy.

Credit John Allyn with sticking to his guns. I know for a fact he could have sold the club for more money to a Seattle group. I saw a Seattle letter calling for more money than Allyn received from the Veeck group.

It wasn't too long after that John died suddenly.

Enter Bill Veeck again. Bill and I went way back to the early 1940s when he and Charlie Grimm ran the Milwaukee club in the minor leagues. Bill had wanted to strike out on his own. He was able to execute some of his own ideas and promotions with the Milwaukee club. And he and Charlie Grimm ran a madcap and successful franchise.

Later, we were both in Marine Corps boot camp. I saw Bill once or twice in San Diego before he had that unfortunate accident that cost him his leg.

He was a real mover, a square peg in the round hole of the establishment and he always had that keen mind and impish sense of humor. He absolutely despised stuffed shirts.

His stunts become legendary. For instance, Bill sent the midget, Eddie Gaedel, up to bat while Veeck was with the St. Louis Browns. Veeck liked to tell the story of how he came upon the idea.

It came from a James Thurber piece in *New Yorker* magazine. It was a story about this midget who got into the World Series. He came to bat and took two strikes. He then swung with all his might and hit a pop fly to second.

Veeck used to recall the story that when he sent Eddie to bat he told him he had an apartment on the top of the stadium and that if Eddie so much as looked like he was going to swing at a pitch, Veeck would shoot him from his perch.

One of Veeck's midget ideas didn't quite work. He had the idea that midget vendors would be great. They could sell and never block the view of the fans. There was only one thing he forgot and that was the weight of the beer trays. The midgets couldn't lift them, much less carry them around the stands.

There were all sorts of Veeck ideas. I loved the one where the helicopter came out of the sky and a group of midgets from Mars captured Nelson Fox and Luis Aparicio and carted them off.

John Hoffman, a writer for the *Chicago Sun-*

Times, says in 30 years he heard Will Harridge, the American League president, use profanity on three occasions. The first time, he said, was so long ago he couldn't remember. The second time was in a private conversation involving Commissioner Happy Chandler and the third time was about that "blankety-blank" midget of Veeck's.

Harridge claimed, and went out of his way to let people know, that the contract of Eddie Gaedel was never processed and, therefore, he never really appeared officially in the American League.

Veeck was great for the city of Chicago, as he was for Cleveland, and he was great for baseball.

Through it all, he never forgot the spirit of baseball and its place in the entertainment world.

Sometimes baseball succeeds in spite of itself. For baseball to suddenly sit back and rest on its laurels and to say that this is ours by divine right, well, then baseball is just looking for trouble.

Veeck always remembered baseball was in the entertainment world and that it had to compete for the entertainment dollars in America.

His roots in Chicago sports history were deep. In the 1930s he was working at Wrigley Field for his dad. Bill received credit for putting the vines up in Wrigley Field.

Later on, he brought a pennant-winner to Chicago—the 1959 White Sox.

Then he came back and operated the club on short money to keep it in Chicago. He held on as long as he could before the financial changes in the game forced him to sell once again.

I know he became very upset with Jerry Reinsdorf and Eddie Einhorn because of some comments attributed to them. Veeck wanted to sell to Edward DeBartolo, but when Veeck had come back into the league the other owners weren't really anxious to have him back. I remember going to an owners' meeting in Cleveland and they set up very tight financial restrictions—knowing in their hearts Veeck couldn't possibly meet the requirements. When he went to sell the club, there were still some dissatisfied owners.

Supposedly, Einhorn irritated Veeck when he and Reinsdorf took control of the club and said that now the ball club would be run in a classy way or words to that effect.

But I don't think Eddie meant it that way. He had nothing to gain by that.

Veeck was always two jumps ahead of the sheriff, but that's the way he liked it. He'd probably have turned down a job as the chief executive of General Motors and a salary in the top 10 in the country.

Einhorn and Reinsdorf brought a new era to Chicago baseball. I think they have done a superb job. Anyone who walks into Comiskey Park and sees all the great changes has to like what these men have done. The Old Roman, Charles Comiskey, built the park to be both a fan's ball park and a players' ball park and he accomplished it. Eddie and Jerry have enhanced it in both regards.

They make a very good team. A few years ago, they came to me with a great contract offer. It was for more money than I ever made before. I thought of it seriously. I can't get angry with anyone who makes that kind of offer. Even though

I stayed with WGN, I didn't use their offer to help negotiations with WGN. I never told WGN about it.

The Wrigley family.

Phil Wrigley was, without any question, one of the most misunderstood men in baseball owners' history. The man had incredible foresight and vision. He was so far ahead of the other owners it was unbelievable.

He warned the owners years and years ago about the reserve clause. No one would listen and look where baseball free agency is today.

He was a man who threatened to pull his club out of the league and play independently if the other owners wouldn't allow him to broadcast his team's games on radio. The other owners said no one would pay to come to games if they got to listen to the games for free. Well, radio turned out to be the salvation of baseball.

With the advent of television, Phil said he wanted to give it a try. His reasoning was the Cubs were drawing a million fans from a pool of 2.5 million. There were many repeaters. He wanted to reach the other 4 million in the Chicagoland area who never came. Maybe television could do it.

One look around the ball parks today shows 40 percent of the fans are women and children. This is possible because television made baseball so visible and made these players seem like part of the family.

I remember negotiating an early television deal with the Cubs.

WGN gave the Cubs $75,000 with the under-
standing that the Cubs would spend $25,000 back
on promotion. Phil Wrigley recognized television
for what it was—a great advertising vehicle for
his ball club. Here's a man who spent millions of
dollars on advertising for his gum company and
knew the value of being in front of the public.

There was a time when the Cubs left WGN
radio and went to WIND. It was before rights fees
and the Cubs were on many different stations in
Chicago. Wrigley was part owner of WIND and
figured it would be the right station for the Cubs.

Plus, WGN was owned by the Mutual Network which featured and sold advertising based
on childrens' shows in the afternoon. Well, the
games started at 3 P.M. in those days and many
times the childrens' shows wouldn't get aired. It's
tough to sell the national advertisers if you can't
deliver the number two market.

So WGN gave up baseball and the Cubs went
to WIND.

When Ward Quaal took over as president and
general manager of the station, Ward had to get
baseball back. Ward loved the game. We did the
Cubs games on television and he wanted baseball
on radio.

I remember being in Phoenix at the Wrigley
estate just off the Biltmore Hotel. I was talking
with the Wrigleys' advertising agency man, Arthur
Meyerhoff.

I told Arthur we were going to make a great
run at the White Sox because we couldn't get the

Cubs. He said, "Wait a minute, there might be a chance to change that situation." A few days later, Meyerhoff contacted me. Wrigley liked the idea of getting a good rights fee and also being on a 50,000 watt station.

The Cubs were already signed with WIND for the next season. We were talking about the following season. Arthur and I put our heads together and came out with a great deal. I told him I was going to make a dramatic shutout bid and offer him a five-year deal for a million dollars. I told Ward Quaal in the first year you may lose a little, in the second year you'll break even, and in the third year you'll make money from then until eternity.

He agreed. The next thing I knew, Ralph Atlass called me from WIND and he said he'd sell the Cubs' rights for the lame duck upcoming season at a cost of $100,000. We jumped at that chance to get the rights immediately. We made money the first year.

Of course, the light issue was almost as strong in Wrigley's time as it is today.

He was very serious about the issue. He said, "Whether or not I object to lights is not the point. When the fans want lights we'll give it to them. I don't oppose lights that much. If I did why would I let my minor league clubs play night games?"

He also said that if someone wanted to build a stadium with lights he would consider playing a dozen or so night games there. But he wouldn't move from Wrigley Field.

Many people thought he didn't care about the Cubs. Nothing could be further from the truth.

When they lost he agonized over it. But he was a shy man. One time he explained to me that the only time he could help the ball club was before the game started or after it was over. Therefore, there was no need for him to attend all the games. Plus, he didn't want to sit high in the mezzanine club box and appear as if he were looking over his kingdom. The lower box made him too accessible for a shy man.

He loved to work with his hands and he had a beautiful workshop at his summer home in Lake Geneva, Wisconsin. He was always working on something, but he was also always listening to the Cubs' games.

One of the better baseball fans in Chicago was Phil's wife, Helen. She loved baseball and the Cubs. She'd attend more games than Phil. Maybe it was because she wasn't as easily recognized.

When Phil and Helen died just months apart, the ramifications were great. Not only on the personal front, but also with regard to the estate. We'll never know how much effect their deaths coming so close to one another had on the estate.

Bill Wrigley took over. His expanded role was not easy. He was a young man with a tremendous amount of pressure. Like his father, Phil, who idolized his father, William, young Bill idolized his father.

Bill had this incredible job. Yet, his primary responsibility was not the ball club, but the gum business and many other company holdings.

He was his own man and when it came to selling the Cubs, he deserves a lot of credit for making sure they were bought by a respected organization. As far as Bill was concerned, he wanted the Cubs to be owned by a responsible company that had a respectable enough image to be good for the ball club. He also didn't want to sell to someone who would hold it for five years and then sell it for a great profit.

I know at least a dozen groups that would have paid more for the Cubs than the price Bill Wrigley received. But he wanted to keep it in Chicago with an outstanding and civic-minded company. That's why he chose the Tribune Company.

I was once offered the job of running the Cubs by Phil Wrigley. I was on the board of directors when some of the Tribune Company lawyers became nervous about the possibility of conflict of interest. They suggested I resign from the board and sell the one share of stock I owned.

Phil accepted the resignation but said as far as he was concerned I would always be a part of the group. He said that I was baseball's greatest salesman. I was always proud of that statement.

One day I was asked to go to Phil's apartment on Lake Shore Drive. He called me in and there were Phil, Arthur Meyerhoff, Bill Wrigley and Bill Hagenah. I wondered what was going on.

Phil asked me if I would be interested in taking over the operations of the ball club. I don't think there's a baseball fan alive who wouldn't like that opportunity and who wouldn't think they could do a good job at it.

I said I was certain I could do it. We kicked the idea around for a while and then he called me and asked if I could work with Leo Durocher as my general manager. He knew that Leo and I weren't the best of friends. But I said I thought I could for the good of the club. He said that's what he expected me to say.

A couple of days later, he did a double take when he learned I still had a year and a half on my WGN contract.

He decided against pursuing it because he didn't want to cause any problems with WGN.

Just about that time I received a call from Bob Kennedy. Bob said he thought he could help the club and wanted to know whom he should contact. I said contact Bill and he did. Next thing you know Bob was the general manager.

In the meantime, I felt that Bill Hagenah was probably the most qualified man to run the club. He turned out to be a very good president of the Cubs.

And then came the Tribune Company.

They have done a great job with the franchise. So far, so good.

The stare of Judge Kenesaw Mountain Landis was piercing.

And, in a way, so was the asterisk left behind by Ford Frick.

Judge Landis struck fear into owners, players and even broadcasters as baseball's first commissioner.

You can look at his photographs and sense that he was not a man to cross.

He was the only man I knew who would cuss for 20 minutes and never repeat himself—he made it sound like poetry.

My first meeting with him came at Wrigley Field. Pat Pieper, the Cubs public address announcer, came over to me and said Judge Landis wanted to see me immediately.

I went over to him with my knees shaking. He looked at me with those piercing eyes and said, "Brickhouse, I've been listening to you and you sound alright. You've been doing a good job. That's all I wanted. Go back to work."

It was quite a first meeting.

Landis was a great commissioner. He ruled very sternly. He was the type of man baseball needed at a crucial time. He was harsh and his authority was never questioned.

There have been commissioners since Landis who ruled with a certain boldness and others who were run by the game.

The commissioner's job has never been easy. The game is forever changing and the issues continue to change with the eras. The commissioner's position is one in which not everyone will always be pleased by the decisions.

Bowie Kuhn is a very good example of a man who wasn't always liked and, at the same time, wasn't always understood.

I believe he did a fine job under some adverse conditions. I think when people look back at his regime they will discover he did as well as could possibly have been done under difficult circumstances.

He was forced to make rulings on new issues that developed from free agency. The Charlie Finley case is a prime example. He overturned a move by Finley that would have sent three of Oakland's better players to the Boston Red Sox and New York Yankees in exchange for a large cash payment. All three players, Joe Rudi, Vida Blue and Rollie Fingers, were about to become free agents, and Charlie knew he would lose them at the end of the season and receive nothing in return.

Kuhn stopped the deal in what he called "the best interests of baseball."

Both men were trying to do what they deemed correct. I also have to admire Finley. Any man who can assemble as many winners as he did has my genuine respect.

Kuhn's tenure was one of turbulence in other areas, too. But I honestly believe he did all he could.

Personally, I had a couple of problems with commissioners.

One was with A.B. "Happy" Chandler.

When Chandler first became commissioner he brought a political perspective with him. Politicians never forgot and sometimes they never forgave even though the essence of politics is tied into the so-called art of compromise.

After some time, he seemed to really begin to understand the business of baseball.

The tremendous revenue generated today by television and radio rights date back to Chandler's days. That source of revenue was inaugurated by him. The numbers pale by today's comparison but, nevertheless, it was Chandler who devised or negotiated the approach that is used today in baseball.

My problem with him concerned my broadcasting of the 1950 All-Star Game. I received word

Chandler had given his approval despite reservations about me.

I couldn't believe it when I heard what he had said. The news stunned me. I wanted to know what he meant. I demanded and received a hearing with him.

He told me when he first took the position as commissioner he heard that I wasn't for him.

I told him I didn't know what he was talking about. I said I didn't know who would have told him that, but that I had adopted a wait-and-see attitude toward his tenure as commissioner.

I told him, "I have absolutely no apology to make for my past and my relationship with Judge Landis. At the same time I have no recollection of ever making any critical remark about you."

I reminded him that I was also aware of his great friendship with Arch Ward of the *Chicago Tribune.* I also told him Ward was a very good friend of mine and there wasn't any way I would have it out with a friend of Ward's.

We shook hands and everything was fine. To this day I wonder what would have happened to my career if I hadn't demanded that we sit down and talk out our difference. He was a man with life-or-death authority over my career as a broadcaster.

Almost the same circumstances developed with Ford Frick. He gave me the okay to do the 1952 All-Star Game in Philadelphia—but I understood that he had his doubts.

At a reception on the eve of the game, he finally told Paul Jonas, the sports director for the Mutual Network, that he was terribly sorry but he had confused me with another broadcaster.

How ironic that Ford Frick and I would become great friends and I should be honored at Cooperstown with the Ford Frick Award.

But make no mistake. Even though we were friends, I did not agree with his placing an asterisk next to the 61 home runs hit by Roger Maris in his record-breaking 1961 season. Maris, of course, had played in more games than Babe Ruth. The schedule had gone from 154 to 162 games.

I didn't buy that decision. If people want to play that asterisk game they could use it in all sports. People can argue both ways. But a superstar is a superstar and he'll be a superstar in any era.

Someone once said to Wendell Smith, the gifted writer and former WGN announcer, that Joe Louis never fought anybody of any renown.

The man said, "Who did Joe Louis ever beat?"

And Wendell replied: "Just everyone they asked him to beat."

What did Roger Maris do? He hit more home runs in a single season than anyone in major league history.

My confrontations with commissioners weren't restricted to baseball. I also had a slight disagreement with Bert Bell of the National Football League.

I broadcast a game in which George Blanda fumbled twice, and late in the game there was a fight.

Later that week, Bert called and told me he would appreciate it if the NFL broadcasters did not deal in negatives.

He said, "Instead of saying the man fumbled the ball say it escaped him."

And he said the league wasn't selling fights, it was selling football.

I asked him, "What was I supposed to say about the fight? Was I to have said they were having a Maypole Dance?"

The phone conversation did become a little heated. But I stuck to my guns. Then again, I was talking to the commissioner of the National Football League.

The next day I went in to see George Halas and asked him if Bert Bell could cost me my job in broadcasting.

Halas looked at me with a funny expression on his face and said he probably could. But then he added, "But I'd never let him."

Any one of the three commissioners could have really put a crimp in my broadcasting career. I wonder how many people never had that talk with someone who disagreed with them and then ended up losing out because of it.

For more than 20 years, Pete Rozelle has been the commissioner of the NFL. He has orchestrated many of the multitude of changes that have changed the picture of a great league.

I first met Pete when he was the public relations director for the Rams. I found him affable and very pleasant. What I didn't see in him was the potential to become the commissioner of a league.

Later, he became the general manager of the Rams. At that point, I could tell his status was increasing.

Pete then became the commissioner, although he was the choice by compromise. Almost immediately after he was named to the position I could see him start to grow. He became the personification of the modern day commissioner.

The early day commissioners were hard-working men who were interested in the development of football. Rozelle was a man who was at the controls when the big business era in sports boomed.

He has a remarkable talent for getting people together. The NFL was two factions—the old-time owners and the new breed. Pete has done a beautiful job of bringing both together and moving them into a new era without losing sight of the debt owed to the long-term owners. As an example, he was considerate of George Halas and all he did for professional football.

In 1963, football and television were still in an early relationship. I remember I visited with Pete before the 1963 title game between the Bears and the New York Giants. I did the national telecast of that game along with Chris Schenkel.

Instead of being at Wrigley Field for the entire game, Rozelle watched at least a portion of the game on closed circuit television. The man was looking ahead in a business-type fashion.

The newest commissioner is baseball's Peter Ueberroth. In a very short period of time he has been faced with some major decisions. He has impressed me with his quick settlement of the umpires' strike during the 1984 post-season. His involvement in the 1985 players' strike also helped avert a major deadlock that could have had damaging ramifications.

His success does not surprise me. And neither will his possible future goals.

A friend of mine, who is an outstanding travel authority, told me at dinner one evening that she had known Peter a very long time through the travel business.

She said it was apparent to her since the first day she had met Ueberroth that Peter wanted to one day become the President of the United States.

Stay tuned.

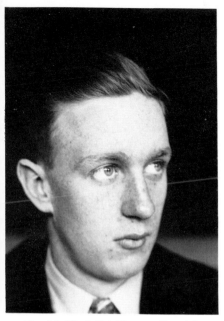

Youthful Jack Brickhouse, Peoria's
"Man on the Street."

Peoria broadcaster Brickhouse lands
an interview with boxing great Joe
Louis.

Bob Elson, "The Commander," helps launch Jack's WGN career.

OF SERVICE

is a full-rate
am or Cable-
unless its de-
character is in-
by a suitable
above or pre-
the address.

WESTERN UNION

1201

(02)

R. B. WHITE
PRESIDENT

NEWCOMB CARLTON
CHAIRMAN OF THE BOARD

J. C. WILLEVER
FIRST VICE-PRESIDENT

SYMBOLS

DL=Day Letter

NL=Night Letter

LC=Deferred Cable

NLT=Cable Night Le

Ship Radiogra

time shown in the date line on telegrams and day letters is STANDARD TIME at point of origin. Time of receipt is STANDARD TIME at point of destin

184 31 DL=ALBUQUERQUE NMEX 14 457P

1940 MAR 14 PM 7 12

CK BROOKHOUSE=

RADIO STATION PEORIA ILL=

E RECOMMENDED YOU FOR OUR ANNOUNCERS STAFF AND SPORTS

SISTANT EXPECT A CALL WIRE ME DEVELOPMENTS TOWN HOUSE

SAN GELES STOP REMEMBER IF ASKED YOU HAVE A THOROUGH

WLEDGE OF BASEBALL REGARDS=

BOB ELSON.

Paul Fogarty, WGN-TV sports producer, chats with Jack Brickhouse, sports service manager and broadcaster for WGN radio and TV in 1948.

Two men at the mike: Jack and colleague Marty Hogan.

Lloyd Pettit, tagged by Brickhouse as "one of the best play-by-play men" he has ever known; Jack; and Jack Rosenberg, WGN sports editor.

Jack with former colleague and Cub broadcaster, Jim West, with whom he worked for six years.

WGN – Prominent names in the station's history: Standing, left to right, Carl Meyers, Jack Brickhouse, Quin Ryan, Bob Elson, and Pierre Andre. Seated is Ward Quaal.

With friend and colleague Milo Hamilton.

Jack with "The Rajah" – Rogers Hornsby.

Scorecard and pencil ready for another day at the ol' ball park.

In between filming for the motion picture *Stage Coach*, Bing Crosby and wife Kathryn talk with Jack at the ball park.

Jack Webb, Sergeant Joe Friday of "Dragnet" fame, takes a break from TV sleuthing to kibitz with Jack and Harry Creighton.

Satchel Paige joins Jack and Lou Boudreau in the booth.

Jack Rosenberg, Jack Brickhouse, Vince Lloyd, and Stan Musial find a lot to smile about during a break in the action at Wrigley Field.

Harry Belafonte visits Eddie Hubbard and Jack at WGN.

Jack gets ready to bring the Cubs into European homes on the first live Telstar Satellite broadcast – July 23, 1962.

Two close for comfort! Jack at ringside, Marigold Gardens, broadcasting head-to-head combat between Al Williams and Tarzan White.

Jack and fellow Chicago Bears broadcaster, Sun-Times columnist Irv Kupcinet.

"Hey-Hey!" and "Sweet-
ness" – Jack and Bears great
running back Walter Payton
in a reflective moment at the
microphone.

Jack and his little daughter Jeanne with another proud dad, Phil Cavarretta, on Father's Day, 1950.

Brickhouse belts a two-bagger (or so he says!) during a benefit softball game. Frank Lane is doing the umpiring.

Hosting "Sports Open Line" as Billy Williams and Alex Agase field questions.

Covering MacArthur Day in Chicago – April 26, 1951.

Gale Sayers, Dick Butkus, and Ron Santo with Jack at a *Sporting News* awards ceremony in 1966.

In his City Hall office, Mayor Daley presents Jack with a bound copy of a Chicago City Council resolution proclaiming ''Jack Brickhouse Day.'' Next to the Mayor is Tom Rosenberg, at that time an alderman, now a judge; looking on is Sid Luckman, once a formidable quarterback for the Chicago Bears.

Jack with Leo Durocher, Ken Holtzman, and Willie Mays.

United Airlines' inaugural flight from Chicago to Hawaii. Giving the DC-8 a civic send-off: Mayor Daley, Jack, and United Airlines' Chairman, William A. Patterson.

Patrick J. O'Malley, Ernie Banks, Jack, Billy Pierce, and Joseph Meegan gather for after-dinner photo session.

A snooze on "Sports Scene" – Jack and Harry Caray exhibit a need for some shuteye.

A memento of the Cubs for Harry's Bar in Paris.

Jack, Bill Veeck, Ray Kroc, and Harry Caray spend some lighthearted moments together.

Proud father Jack congratulates daughter Jeanne upon her graduation from Augustana College, 1971.

Receiving the accolades of the Wrigley Field faithful on the occasion of his 5000th broadcast, August 5, 1979.

"I Got the Horse Right Here" – Brickhouse with his four-legged namesake.

Enjoying a laugh with friends in celebration of his 5000th broadcast.

Governor James Thompson and Mayor Jane Byrne congratulate Jack on his 5000th broadcast.

Induction at Cooperstown: Jack joins baseball's immortals in the Hall of Fame, July 1983.

A gathering of legends: Chicago Sports Hall of Fame 1983 inductees. Top row, left to right: Jack McHugh, Bill DeCorrevont, Jack, Nat "Sweetwater" Clifton, Johnny "Red" Kerr, Elmer Angsman. Bottom row, left to right: Edmund Kelly, Henny Young, accepting for his brother, Buddy Young, Johnny Lattner, Marshall Goldberg, Jay Berwanger, Billy Pierce.

"Pomp and Circumstance" for Dr. John B. Brickhouse. Wife Pat congratulates Jack for Honorary Doctor of Laws degree presented by the National College of Education, July 1985.

Jack and Pat Brickhouse in a special moment with Pope Paul VI.

Jack and wife Pat with former President Jerry Ford.

Sportscaster to sportscaster: Jack has a fireside chat with President Reagan, who broadcast Cub games by ticker in the 30s.

Jack poses with Wrigley Field plaque, presented to him by the Chicago Cubs in commemoration of broadcasting 5000 games, April 1940 to August 1979, on WGN.

VII

Highlights—and 1969

I claim one all-time record: I have telecast the play-by-play on eight no-hit, no-run games in the major leagues.

Here's the rundown:

1955 — Sam (Toothpick) Jones, Cubs vs. Pittsburgh, May 12, 4-0

1960 — Don Cardwell, Cubs vs. St. Louis, May 15, 4-0

1965 — Jim Maloney, Cincinnati vs. Cubs, August 19, 1-0 (10 innings)

1967 — Joel Horlen, White Sox vs. Detroit, September 10, 6-0

1969 — Ken Holtzman, Cubs vs. Atlanta, August 19, 3-0

1971 — Ken Holtzman, Cubs vs. Cincinnati, June 3, 1-0

1972 — Burt Hooton, Cubs vs. Philadelphia, April 16, 4-0

1972 — Milt Pappas, Cubs vs. San Diego, September 2, 8-0

Ironically, seven of the eight no-hitters were turned in by Chicago pitchers—six Cubs, one Sox.

Seven of the eight were pitched in Chicago. The lone exception: Holtzman's second no-hitter at Cincinnati.

I never have telecast a perfect game.

The Cubs were involved in one at Los Angeles on September 9, 1965, when the Dodgers' Sandy Koufax was letter perfect. WGN Television didn't carry that game. Vince Lloyd and Lou Boudreau experienced the thrill of doing it on WGN Radio and, I might add, did themselves proud with a memorable job.

The closest I came to telecasting a perfect game was on September 2, 1972. Milt Pappas of the Cubs was one out away against San Diego but walked pinch-hitter Larry Stahl on a 3-2 pitch.

Pappas will insist forever that ball four to Stahl was in the strike zone.

The umpire behind the plate that day was Bruce Froemming. Pappas encountered him at a banquet the following winter. Milt said: "You know in your heart that was a strike. Just think, both of us would have been famous."

Froemming retorted: "If I called a pitch like that a strike, I wouldn't be able to sleep nights."

Answered Pappas: "Then how in the hell do you sleep all those other nights when you blow those calls?"

In any case, the difference between pitching a perfect game as compared to a regular no-hitter cost Pappas a lot of money in endorsements and salary.

One other near-perfect game I recall vividly came at New York in 1969. The Mets' Tom Seaver had gone eight and a third innings without permitting a Cubs' baserunner at Shea Stadium, but Jimmy Qualls ruined it all with a single.

My first no-hit telecast, in 1955, bordered on

the incredible. Sam (Toothpick) Jones, blessed with a fantastic curveball but wild much of the day, carried the drama to the hilt against Pittsburgh by walking the bases full to start the top of the ninth.

Manager Stan Hack of the Cubs went to the mound. The Cubs were leading, 4-0, and Hack gave Jones the unvarnished word: "One more walk and I'm taking you out, no-hitter or not."

Jones proceeded to strike out the side.

He got Frank Thomas on a called third strike on a 3-2 count to end it.

Thomas will insist forever that strike three was not in the strike zone.

Some 4,000 fans saw that game. But over the years, I've run into 20,000 who said they were there.

By the same token, I've covered some games which had 20,000 attendance, but today I wouldn't be able to find 4,000 who would admit they were there!

When Jones completed his no-hitter, Harry Creighton, my talented sidekick, rushed onto the field for an on-the-spot interview. His first question: "Sam, how's the family?"

That had to be one of the greatest lines in sports broadcasting history.

A day or so later, Creighton interviewed Jones on a pre-game show and presented Toothpick Sam with a lasting memento: a gold toothpick.

The boys in press row kidded Creighton after that.

They claimed Sam Jones' teeth had turned green!

I cannot recall ever seeing a man throw a baseball harder than did Don Cardwell in his no-hitter against the Cardinals in 1960.

It was Cardwell's first start for the Cubs after being traded away by the Phillies. He threw smoke. I covered Bob Feller and Koufax and the other flame-throwers for years but on this one given day Cardwell was fastest of all.

At that, his no-hitter almost disappeared with two out in the ninth. Joe Cunningham of St. Louis hit a sinking liner to left but Walt (Moose) Moryn raced in to take that ball off a tall blade of grass and preserve the masterpiece.

Cincinnati's Jim Maloney was forced to go 10 innings before completing his 1-0 no-hitter over the Cubs on August 19, 1965. Two months earlier, Maloney had pitched 10 no-hit innings against the New York Mets. Then he lost the whole works in the 11th on a home run by Johnny Lewis.

Joel Horlen pitched the lone White Sox no-hitter of my telecasting career. That was in 1967. It was the first game of a doubleheader with Detroit. The second game, naturally, was anti-climactic. I don't even remember who won.

What I do remember about Horlen's gem is that the Tigers' Jerry Lumpe almost beat out an infield roller in the ninth, an eyelash play at first.

Let's face it, I guess the ninth innings of all no-hitters are pulsating.

Kenny Holtzman was a fine strikeout pitcher but his first no-hitter—that was against Atlanta in 1969—was accomplished without a single strikeout. It has to be the only no-hitter in the books with that unusual statistic.

Ron Santo's three-run homer in the first provided two more runs than Holtzman needed.

In the seventh, Henry Aaron slammed a towering fly ball to left. I hollered, immediately: "And there goes the no-hitter."

That ball, believe it or not, hung over Waveland Avenue for an instant, then was forced back by a strong north wind. Somehow, Billy Williams, playing left, had refused to give up on it—and he made the catch near the curvature in the wall.

Nothing could stop Holtzman after that.

Holtzman simply mowed down powerful Cincinnati to record his second no-hitter in 1971, the first to be thrown in Riverfront Stadium. Lee May struck out to end the game on what may have been the fastest fastball of Holtzman's life.

Burt Hooton, using the knuckle curve as his phantom pitch, came in with his no-hitter over the Phillies on the first Sunday of the 1972 season. Hooton survived an episode similar to Holtzman's. Greg Luzinski socked one to center that apparently was a home run, but the wind ruled otherwise and the ball blew back for a routine out.

Eight no-hit telecasts.

Am I growing old?

I was privileged to do the network television or radio on five All-Star games and four World Series.

My first All-Star assignment came in 1950. The National League won it on Red Schoendienst's 14th inning home run after Ralph Kiner had smacked one in the ninth to tie it at Comiskey Park.

That was the game in which Ted Williams fractured his elbow when he ran into the outfield wall. He was out for the rest of the season. His teammate, Billy Goodman, went on to win the American League batting title.

The chance to telecast that game probably was a turning point in my career. It brought me to the attention of the network people.

The World Series always brought with it a fresh, exciting feeling. Every World Series is historic, but some plays will live in my memory forever.

I was broadcasting for two such plays — defensive gems that proved pivotal to the series champions.

The greatest World Series I was ever associated with was the 1952 confrontation between the Brooklyn Dodgers and the New York Yankees.

In the seventh game, the Yankees led Brooklyn, 4-2. It was the seventh inning and the Dodgers loaded the bases. Jackie Robinson was batting with a full count. The runners were going on the pitch.

Robinson lofted a high infield fly. It was first baseman Joe Collins' play. Apparently, he lost sight of the ball. The Yankee pitcher, Bob Kuzava, didn't move.

Billy Martin made a dash from his second base

position and made the catch ankle high to stop the rally. By the time Martin made the catch, two Dodger baserunners had crossed the plate.

That play killed the Dodgers.

It was two years later when I broadcast the most famous catch in World Series history.

The New York Giants were playing the Cleveland Indians in the Polo Grounds in Game 1.

Vic Wertz was the batter. The score was tied 2-2 and the Indians had two runners on base. Don Liddle was the pitcher for New York as the Indians batted in the eighth inning.

Wertz hit a drive to deep center field. Mays raced back and with his back to the infield reached out to grab the ball 460 feet from the plate. The Giants went on to win the game 5-2 in 10 innings.

The Indians, winners of a league record 111 games, never recovered. The Giants swept Cleveland in four games.

The catches by Martin and Mays rank as two of the greatest plays in World Series history. I broadcast both—one that travelled 60 feet and another that landed 460 feet from home plate.

In 1959, the White Sox ended a 40-year drought.

The game that clinched the pennant was played in Cleveland. Al Lopez called on Gerry Staley to pitch to Vic Power in the ninth. Staley threw one pitch to Power. The ball was hit on the ground. Luis Aparicio stepped on second base for one out and threw to first to complete the double play. The White Sox had won the pennant with a team that scratched for runs, played air-tight defense and utilized brilliant pitching.

The city of Chicago erupted. One thrill led to another that season.

I telecast the World Series with Vin Scully. We earned the *Look Magazine* Award for our efforts.

The fifth game of the Series was played in the Los Angeles Coliseum in front of 92,706 fans, the largest baseball crowd to date.

It was a crucial game for the White Sox. They trailed the Dodgers three games to one. The Sox survived Game 5 with a 1-0 victory.

The only run came off Sandy Koufax. Nelson Fox singled in the fourth inning. He advanced to third on a single by Jim Landis and scored on a double play ball hit by Sherm Lollar.

Al Lopez made one of the timeliest defensive moves of the season during the eighth inning. With Charlie Neal at bat, Lopez called time. He moved Al Smith from right field to left and put Jim Rivera in right.

Within seconds, Neal ripped a pitch into right field. Rivera made a sensational catch to preserve the victory and make Lopez look like a genius. In any event, the Dodgers took the Series in six games.

The number one plum in college football is the Rose Bowl. I have been to a pair of Rose Bowl games.

In 1944, I was in the Marine Corps and stationed in San Diego. I had a couple days leave and hitchhiked to Pasadena. I sat in the end zone and watched Southern Cal beat Washington, 29-0.

It was eight years before I went to my second

Rose Bowl game. I travelled a different route than I did in 1944. In 1952, I was broadcasting the game on national television and I was driven to the game in a limousine.

I must admit the second experience was a slight improvement compared to my first trip to Pasadena.

Illinois defeated Stanford, 40-7. Mel Allen and I broadcast the game. We flipped a coin to decide who would work which half. I lost the flip but was able to broadcast the better half—the first half. Stanford led 7-6 at the intermission. It wasn't much of a game after the first 10 minutes of the second half.

I am not sure what this indicates about the luck of a coin toss but I do know that it was more fun to go to a bowl game as a broadcaster than it was as a Marine.

All right, I've put it off long enough. It's time to face the question: Where did the 1969 Chicago Cubs go wrong?

I would like to be able to lay the full blame on Manager Leo Durocher, but realistically, that would be unfair.

That Leo did more than his share to help lose the pennant goes without question.

He lost control of the Cubs in '69.

In the final analysis, though, I think the New York Mets simply had a better baseball team than the Cubs.

They caught lightning in a bottle and knew what to do with it. If ever there was a Team of Destiny, it had to be the Miracle Mets.

Even now, years later, as I pour these words into a tape recorder, I look at an old National League Green Book and there written in what appears to be blood is a notation I still find difficult to believe:

FINAL STANDINGS

NL East			Games Behind
New York	100	62	. . . . .
Chicago	92	70	8

On August 13, 1969, the Mets, managed by Gil Hodges, were third and apparently out of it, 9½ games behind the first-place Cubs.

They then won 22 of the next 28 to move into the lead on September 10. They then won 16 of the next 21 to take division honors going away. Next, they won three straight from Atlanta in the playoffs. Finally, they won the World Series, four games to one, over Baltimore.

One of the Mets, J. C. Martin, was to tell me later that the New Yorkers suspected they were a team of destiny on September 12. That's when they went into Pittsburgh and swept a double-header by identical scores of 1-0 and their pitchers, Jerry Koosman and Don Cardwell, drove in the only runs. A few nights later, the Mets suffered 19 strikeouts against Steve Carlton in St. Louis but they bailed out, 4-3, on a pair of two-run homers by Ron Swoboda.

I was heartsick when the Cubs blew it.

I was heartsick, in particular, for Phil Wrigley. He deserved that pennant. He had dreamed of one since 1945.

Yet, I'm certain if you asked each and every player to take a lie detector test and posed the question, "Did you give that season everything you had?," they would all answer "yes" and it would be the truth.

They gave it everything they had. But in the end it just wasn't enough.

Sure they fooled around a lot and cut a record and did some other off-the-field ventures. But that didn't hurt the club.

This was a team with Ernie Banks, Glenn Beckert, Don Kessinger and Ron Santo in the infield. And Billy Williams and Jim Hickman in the outfield with Randy Hundley catching and a pitching staff that included Fergie Jenkins, Bill Hands, Ken Holtzman and Phil Regan. Those were All-Star players. Great players in their time—the class of an era.

Many people pointed to the Don Young incident in New York in July as a pivotal time. Young, a rookie centerfielder, dropped a fly ball during an afternoon game. The Mets used the error to rally and beat the Cubs.

After the game, Young, being young and embarrassed, left the locker room as soon as possible and Santo, the captain, exploded.

He thought Young was indifferent. Santo really blasted him.

Well, in the middle of the night, Santo realized what he had done. He called the reporters and apologized to Young.

The next day I was sitting on the team bus waiting to go to the park. I was sitting behind Young. Santo got on and sat on the armrest of

Young's seat and put his arm around the kid and apologized once more. Durocher also put the blast on the kid and we're still waiting for Leo to apologize.

The team knew it was simply a case of a kid dropping the ball. The season was only at the midway point and the Cubs would hold a huge lead for more than another month before the Mets would step out and win it.

But let's face it, the Cubs were a ragtag team in the stretch, wandering aimlessly, with assorted regulars physically exhausted as the result of failure to get a day off here and there when their lead was commanding. That had to be Leo's responsibility and he added fuel to the fire with the tensions he created by nit-picking controversies with certain of his players and certain members of the media.

Pittsburgh started the Cubs toward the deep end in a late season game at Wrigley Field. The Cubs led, 5-4, in the top of the ninth, two out, none on. Willie Stargell hit one out off Phil Regan. The Pirates went on to win in extra innings.

Things went to pieces after that.

Leo got the Cubs' job in 1966. The Wrigley family sounded out a number of people, including me, before making the move. I endorsed Durocher. I knew of his stormy background but I had seen his leadership ability first-hand over the years.

I was to learn later the game had passed him by. That had nothing to do with his age. Some men are old at 30, others are young at 65.

He came to Chicago and at the first press conference made one ill-famed comment: "The Cubs," he said, "are definitely not an 8th place team."

He was right. They finished 10th.

In the meantime, I was instrumental in lining him up with a radio-television package at WGN. He was to get $22,500 and the use of a car for appearing once every-other-week on a television show called "Sports Open Line," working radio with Lou Boudreau on "Durocher In The Dugout" before each Cubs' game and making a handful of personal appearances.

The ink had just dried on the contract when Leo told me he needed an advance on his salary. Charlie Gates, then station manager at WGN Radio, okayed an advance of $12,500. Durocher was very appreciative. Shortly thereafter, he said he needed the other $10,000. The station came through again. Now Leo was overjoyed. Within six weeks, he had been paid off in full on a year's contract, an incredible happening in our industry.

I will say this: Leo Durocher was a genuine expert on that microphone. He was provocative to be sure, and he didn't care whose toes he stepped on, but at the same time he had a certain charisma. He was very quotable and at times probably didn't let the facts stand in the way of an otherwise good story.

He used pet expressions—"he came to play"—"he came to kill ya"—"some kind of second baseman"—"some kind of arm"—and yet he claimed that his most quotable quote of all—"nice guys finish last"—had been taken out of context years earlier.

In any case, WGN paid him $25,000 the second year but Leo came in with an attorney the third year and wanted the amount jacked up considerably. Local stations simply can't pay that kind of money to part-time announcers. So our television side dropped him. He kept "Durocher In The Dugout" on radio at a lesser figure. I think he brooded about the loss of the television deal. Maybe he blamed me. He shouldn't have because during his regime here, I was responsible for getting him at least a total of $100,000 in extra money between the aforementioned station deals and outside commercial commitments.

Leo claimed he never read the newspapers, yet he always seemed to know who had taken a whack at him. I honestly feel he enjoyed any kind of publicity, good or bad, and there can be no doubt he was a real newsmaker.

I won't deny he was partially responsible, at least, for the surge in Cubs' attendance in the late 1960s.

I am uncertain as to why and how Leo and I had our falling out.

I do know he had a stooge or two who would monitor my telecasts and report back to him with anything that remotely sounded like a second guess. He would needle me, I would retort and after a while I simply avoided visiting his office.

Leo claimed the fact that I wasn't invited to his wedding reception, when he married Lynn Goldblatt, rankled me. My answer to that was, "Leo never invites me to his weddings." However, he did manage to invite my big boss, Ward Quaal, then the president of WGN, with whom he had only a passing acquaintance. In fact, Quaal's name was misspelled on the invitation.

I fully realize it is every man's prerogative to ask the friends of his choice to his own wedding reception. But I felt he went out of his way to slight me and the rest of the broadcasters and sportswriters who covered his exploits daily.

I objected to the way Leo handled Ernie Banks. He disliked Ernie from the go. It was just that Ernie was too big a name in Chicago to suit Durocher. Ernie Banks was and is the most popular athlete ever to put on a uniform in this city and I am positive Leo objected to Ernie's tremendous popularity with the fans.

He did his best, I felt, to break down Ernie's spirit, but no man can break a spirit like that.

I remember the game, at the tail end of Banks' career, that he let Ernie bat against a sidearming right-hander, then put in another right-handed hitter, Jim Hickman, as a pinch-hitter for Banks with a left-hander on the mound. Hickman told me later it was one of the toughest things he ever had to do.

In 1970, the Cubs closed out the season at New York and it appeared that this would be Banks' final game as a player. Leo withheld him from the lineup. It was a slap in the face. The fact that Ernie wound up making token appearances in 1971 is beside the point.

Well, I guess all that stuff is water over the dam now. To this day, I still don't send Leo a Christmas card. That makes us even. He doesn't send me one, either. No way.

VIII
Presidents and A Pope

I have been fortunate, very fortunate.

My life has revolved around sports, the toy department in the media business.

There are thousands of men and women who would cherish the opportunities I have had and the memories I have accumulated. For years, wherever I went people would stop and ask me about sports. Sports is the outlet people look forward to after working all day and worrying about life's problems. I was always privileged to work in an area of entertainment and enjoyment. I never forgot that.

While my career will always be tied tightly to the sports world, I learned early there was more to life than sports.

I was able to change course through the winter months after the baseball and football seasons ended.

For years I did a show "Jack Brickhouse Reports." The world was my beat. It recharged my spirit, freshened my approach after the day-in, day-out rigors of a baseball and football season.

Experiences of that nature are very special.

Through the years, I not only dealt with the

superstars of sports, but also with the "superstars" of politics, religion and Hollywood.

I had my share of highlights and also a few somber moments—like the late afternoon of April 12, 1945. Word came that day from Warm Springs, Georgia that Franklin Delano Roosevelt, the 32nd President of the United States, had died.

I was working the 5 O'Clock News on WGN Radio. It was about twenty minutes to five. I was in the studio looking over my copy. Lee Bennett was doing his record show. Vaguely, I heard someone say, "I refuse to announce it without the copy. Maybe Brickhouse will do it. He can do it without the copy." With that, Lee handed me the hot line phone to the news room in the next building.

Suddenly, all hell broke loose. Someone yelled, "For God's sake, Jack, get it on the air. President Roosevelt has died at Warm Springs, Georgia."

It was a chilling feeling. When something like that happens, there is a certain electricity that takes over the studio.

The control room quickly filled with engineers. Now I had to ad lib, with no copy, the death of the President of the United States.

I went on the air and reported, "Ladies and gentlemen, President Franklin D. Roosevelt has just died at his home in Warm Springs, Georgia."

As much as I wanted the President to be alive, I was desperately hoping the facts I was given were correct.

I looked up in the control room and there was concern on everyone's face. What a moment that was.

I also have other memories of Roosevelt.

In 1936 President Roosevelt came to central Illinois. He visited Bloomington on a whistle stop. In those days, Bloomington had a population of about 30,000. There must have been 50,000 people at the depot.

Since I was in Peoria, just 40 miles away, I went over for the speech and managed to get a good position near the end car – the car from which the President would speak.

Roosevelt had a special handrail on each side of the back platform that allowed him to stand erect. He came out and gripped the handrail so that he wouldn't tire so easily.

Like every train station, the name of the town was on the side of the depot except in this case there was a group of men standing on a baggage cart blocking out the President's view of the last three letters in Bloomington. So he began his speech by saying, "My friends from" – and you could see him searching for the sign – "My friends from Bloomingburg, it gives me great pleasure to be here. I'm counting on you for all your support." Well, he gambled and lost with the name.

While on assignment in Washington to cover the 1945 inauguration of President Roosevelt, I had my picture taken with the President at the south portico of the White House.

A month later, Ed Kelly, the Chicago mayor, was at WGN. I asked Ed if it was possible to have the President autograph the photo. He told me it wouldn't be a problem and directed me on the proper people to contact. He added I should wait a few days before sending the photo to Washington because the President would be out of town.

A full 24 hours later, the news broke. President Roosevelt was on the way to Yalta in the Crimea where he joined Winston Churchill and Joseph Stalin in one of the world's most historic conferences. The Crimea Declaration, which emerged from the conference, affirmed the principles of the Atlantic Charter and the objectives of the Casablanca conference. The conference also produced the plans for the defeat of Germany in World War II and set up a future meeting in San Francisco at which the United Nations would be organized as an enduring international structure.

The conference had been a secret from the press until the actual announcement. However, Kelly was aware of it for at least a day before the event took place. It showed the strength of the relationship between Kelly and Roosevelt.

At the inauguration, I was broadcasting for the Mutual Network. I was stationed in a very good position in relation to the podium where the President accepted the oath of office.

Bob Trout, the CBS announcer, was behind me while NBC and ABC broadcasters were on the opposite side of the podium.

As the ceremony proceeded, Trout began inching forward. I inched a little farther forward. He inched closer. I inched closer.

I looked at him and whispered, "I'll lay 8-to-5 I can beat you to him."

Trout gave me a disparaging look and retreated.

Just prior to that near confrontation, I was disturbed by a South American network which was broadcasting in Spanish.

They had been positioned several feet from

my station. I couldn't understand what was being said, but I could certainly hear it loud and
clear.

I gave them a couple of glances and asked
them to please speak softer. Finally, I said, "Do
you understand English?"

They nodded. I then told them to either move
or shut up.

In a split second, a towering security man approached us and in hushed tones asked if there
was anything wrong.

We understood there wouldn't be anything
wrong from that point.

The South American station went back to its
position and continued in relative silence. The
Presidential Inauguration took place without a
hitch.

It has been well-chronicled that back in the
1930s, Ronald Reagan was a sports announcer at
WHO in Des Moines. He used to broadcast Cubs'
games off ticker tape reports. So I felt it would be
no problem to line up President Reagan for a baseball interview to feature on our Cubs' spring training television preview in March of '81. I was wrong.

White House media consultants worried that
if the President granted me a baseball interview,
he then would have to accommodate every other
major league broadcaster.

It looked like no deal until I contacted Con-
gressman Bob Michel, the Peoria Republican. He
came through and a handful of days later, there
I was, interviewing the President in the family din-
ing room of the White House.

It was another case where persistency had paid off.

I was told the interview could not exceed two minutes because of the President's busy schedule. We wound up talking 11 minutes—and he took a certain pride in saying he was still a frustrated Cubs' fan.

I always wanted to do a tape-recorded audience with Pope Paul VI. It was when I had my show "Jack Brickhouse Reports." I arranged it through Joe Meegan of the Back of the Yards Council in Chicago. Joe put me in touch with Monsignor Paul Marcinkus, who is now a bishop. One of the finest men I have ever met. The year was 1965.

Marcinkus arranged it in Rome and he told me that rather than attend the big audience at St. Peter's Square, he suggested a smaller audience. On Wednesday, there was a much more intimate audience for about 1,500 people. I said that was fine.

I came with my tape recorder. They (the security people) looked me over. They didn't catch my tape recorder going in. Thanks to Father Marcinkus, I was right at the foot of the throne. I had done a lot of taping already of the day's festivities when suddenly, while waiting for the Pope's arrival, a member of the Papal plain clothes detective service saw me holding the tape recorder.

He tried to get it away from me. I didn't understand Italian and he didn't understand English. What we both understood is that each one of us wanted the tape recorder. I thought we were going to get into a wrestling match right there. There was no way I would let go of that tape recorder and he was thinking there was no way he would let me keep it.

Suddenly, the doors opened and the Pope made his appearance. The Processional followed. They got to the throne and as Father Marcinkus walked by he realized what was going on and nodded to the detective that everything was all right.

The man had to back off. That he did, but not once did he take his eyes off me. The audience was fantastic. It was so very special.

I got it all on tape and I wouldn't let it out of my sight. I brought it back to the States and took it to Father John Banahan, who was in charge of radio and television for the Chicago Archdiocese.

I told John of my situation. I needed the tape translated into English. He said that he knew Paul Marcinkus and he'd be delighted to help.

He made it a class project for his students. They translated it beautifully.

Paul (Red) Rusdorf, one of the great engineers, put together a 30-minute tape and we made it into a broadcast on Palm Sunday and repeated it for the Catholic school system children. We made it into an album and gave it to the Church.

Still later, Jim Hanlon, then the publicity director of WGN, submitted the tape to Barcelona, Spain and the Ondas Awards. The Ondas Award is from a publishing company in Spain that gives broadcast awards.

And what do you know, it won. I was very

proud of that. The only international award ever at WGN and the old sportscaster got it for them.

During the 1964 convention in San Francisco, I had just finished an interview with Dwight D. Eisenhower. The interview was over and the microphones shut down.

I said, "Off the record, Mr. President, I understand that if you check the box scores of a certain pro baseball league in a small Kansas town you will find a certain player playing right field named D. Brown who is really Dwight Eisenhower."

He looked at me and said, "Where the hell did you get that?"

Well, he went on to say it was true.

"This fellow," the President said, "offered three of us a chance to play ball and earn a couple dollars while keeping our college eligibility."

It was common practice in those days.

One of the things about political conventions is the one-liners you come up with.

In 1964, I got an interview with Bill Miller, who was the Vice-Presidential candidate and Barry Goldwater's running mate.

He said, "I'm a Roman Catholic and Barry Goldwater is Episcopalian and Jewish. Anyone who votes against this ticket is a bigot."

In 1960, I covered the convention in Los Angeles. That was the Democratic Convention that nominated John F. Kennedy. Harry Truman was there and decided to stir things up by proclaiming that the convention was rigged for Senator Kennedy. He was just trying to put a little fight into the convention. The press played it up big.

I had an interview with Jim Farley, who had been Roosevelt's campaign manager. I asked him his reaction to Truman's claim the convention was rigged in favor of Senator Kennedy. He said, "Well, now, as one who has rigged one or two myself, what's wrong with it?"

In 1975, Ronald Reagan was running against Gerald Ford in the primary. Reagan was in Kalamazoo, Michigan. I was sent to cover him. At that time there was a lot of conversation about a Ford-Reagan ticket. I've seen it happen before where two men totally opposite of each other get together on one ticket for the good of the party. It happened with Reagan and George Bush and with John F. Kennedy and Lyndon Johnson.

So I asked Reagan if he would consider being Ford's Vice-President if the party came to him and told him it was for the good of the party.

He looked at me and said, "Jack, it's been my experience only the lead dog gets a change of scenery. No, I don't think I'll go for that."

One of my proudest moments was an exclusive interview I had with Richard Nixon.

W. Clement Stone was one of the major contributors to the party and he had a few favors coming. He decided to collect one of those favors for me.

Long before the convention in Miami Beach, everyone knew Nixon would be the candidate. I wanted to interview Nixon for WGN radio and television and I wanted an exclusive.

Understand now that politicians are normally running all over each other trying to get press coverage nearly all the time. The only time they don't seem to want it is at conventions. They're in the public eye there and they're somebody, they're hot and suddenly they start to play the network game.

At a convention there are maybe as many as 300 radio and television stations. As big and as powerful as WGN is, it is just one of many large and powerful independents.

I had one advantage in that if it's between Jack Brickhouse and a lesser known announcer, I'll get the interview. Sports has put my name in the spotlight. That's why the company sent me to conventions.

I wanted to get Nixon for WGN, but I knew I needed to go to work on this a long time before, so I went to Clement Stone and he helped put it together.

He came back and said Nixon would do this for me and WGN. He said he'd give us an interview after he was nominated.

Bob Foster of our Washington Bureau and I ended up stashing ourselves and a crew on the 17th floor of the Playboy Hotel in Miami. After Nixon was nominated and finished his press conference with everyone, he was going to walk down the hall and down a flight of stairs into our room and be interviewed for WGN.

When Herb Klein, Nixon's press chief, heard this he was furious. Now he had to placate the networks. Klein contacted me and asked if I'd please forget about the request. I said there was no way I was not going to see this through. He asked if we would settle for the chance to ask one question in the main press conference.

I said, "No. My idea is not to have the back of my head on camera and be a voice in the darkness. I'm holding you to the promise Nixon made." I stuck to my guns.

I had my camera crew ready at 6 P.M. even though it would be hours before they were needed. Sure enough, Nixon was nominated and came down the hall, down the flight of stairs and stepped into our room for an interview on WGN radio and television. He did a four to five minute exclusive.

He left our room, went down the hall and named Spiro Agnew as his running mate. I'm very proud of that interview. I saw Herb Klein a few years later. We shook hands. We both knew each of us was just trying to do his job.

I was very surprised by the trouble Nixon had with Watergate. Dick Daley was one of my good friends long before he became mayor of Chicago. I did a show called "Marriage License Romances" from his office when he was the County Clerk. We'd interview couples taking out their marriage licenses. So I knew Dick for many years.

Now, he's mayor and we were at a banquet. He used to love to talk sports. Every time we'd be together he'd ask me about the White Sox and the Cubs and the Bears. Sure enough we're sitting together and he was asking me about sports.

When we were finished I asked him about Watergate.

Now keep in mind, here was one of the shrewdest political minds who ever lived. The man was a political genius.

He said, "Jack, if I live to be 1,000 years old I will never understand the stupidity of the Republican Party in letting Watergate become anything more than an incident. Incidents happen every day. Why did these people play it so stupidly? I can't believe my ears and eyes."

I was in Paris at a time when Richard Burton was working in the movie *The Comedian* with Alec Guinness, David Niven, and Gloria Foster.

Peter Ustinov had been a friend of mine for a long time. He called Richard and arranged the interview for me. It didn't hurt that my mother was born in Cardiff, Wales.

One of my questions to him was why would someone with a good rugby background be interested in an American sport like baseball.

And he said that he had been working in *Camelot* on Broadway. At the end of the show the stage manager presented him with a book on baseball. Richard said that the two had argued long and hard about the merits of rugby versus baseball.

The book he received was the equivalent of a baseball primer. He said he was fascinated by the intricacies of the game. He found himself drawing diagrams of plays and experimenting with strategies.

So time passed and he returned to New York to do *Hamlet*. Elizabeth Taylor and he were living in a New York apartment. He said one Sunday, Elizabeth said to him as he was watching the Mets on television, "Is that all you can do on a nice day is watch that bloody baseball?"

Richard replied, "A good wife would be interested in her husband's interests. Sit down here with me. And besides, dear, it's already the eighth inning and it's almost over."

On this particular day, the Mets and the Pittsburgh Pirates played 23 innings. To somebody who loves the game it was fantastic. To someone who doesn't know the game, there was this dreadful monotony.

In the 16th or 17th inning she said she was leaving.

Richard told me, "I had a tough time selling her on the sport after that."

Then a few years later they were on the West Coast making *Who's Afraid of Virginia Woolf?*. Elizabeth was interested in watching the Dodgers and Maury Wills because of Wills' ability to steal bases. She nicknamed him "Sneaky."

Richard told me Liz was interested in the Dodgers and Wills and I told him that the Dodgers had just traded Maury to the Pirates. Suddenly Burton was a typical fan.

He looked at me and said, "Damndest mistake they ever could make."

IX

Of Golf and the Galloping Ghost

I should have suspected, even at age 12, that I would get hooked on the frustrating game of golf and, at times, get hooked by it, too.

There I was, a new caddie at Mt. Hawley Country Club in Peoria, carrying the sticks of kindly theatre executive Len Worley. It was the 14th hole, and Mr. Worley sliced his second shot. Another golfer, coming the other way on the 15th fairway, sliced his shot simultaneously.

The balls collided in mid-air.

That bizarre happenstance probably established the trend for my own golf game. I have never known what to expect next.

Beginning caddies earned 20 cents an hour in those days, veterans a quarter, and we used to hope that course traffic would be slow enough to enable us to earn a dollar for an 18-hole round.

Little did I realize back then that years later I would receive an honorary membership at Mt. Hawley.

It can now be written that I have played golf all over the world. You name a particular hole at a particular course and it's 6-to-5 I have double-bogeyed it.

Even though my handicap at one point of a lackluster links career was an honest 12, I have lacked consistency with the following clubs: 2-iron, 3-iron, 4-iron, 5-iron, 6-iron, 7-iron, 8-iron, 9-iron, pitching wedge, sand wedge, putter, driver, 3-wood and 4-wood.

I have been known to belt a 5-iron 150 yards to within four feet of the pin, then carefully take three putts to drop it.

My temperament and temperature have risen and fallen in accordance with my score.

I hereby apologize for all of my golf course profanities over the years. But I insist that any normal, decent, clean-living American would have uttered the same words if he had butchered the same holes.

Or as I tell the boys at Ridgemoor, I refuse to acknowledge a man's golfing ability until I see whether he can sink a two-foot putt with $100 riding on it. Remember, you heard it here first.

I sympathize with Ken Venturi's story about the hotheaded golfer who finished off a miserable round with a 7 on the par-4 18th. He took his clubs, bag and all, and threw them into a water hole, then stormed off to the parking lot.

He realized suddenly that his car keys were in the bag. So he returned to the 18th, took off his shoes, waded into the water, retrieved the bag, carefully opened the zipper, removed the keys, closed the zipper—and pitched the set back into the drink again!

Two columns, both of which appeared in the

Chicago Tribune, offer insights into my life and times at golf. Here's what Cooper Rollow wrote:

The question I am about to bring up does not rank as one of the burning social issues of our time, so relax. This is a "fun" column because it deals with Jack Brickhouse, and who is more fun to pick on than WGN's genial voice of the Chicago Cubs?

The question I submit for your consideration on this August Sunday is as follows: Is Jack Brickhouse really the pleasant, mild-mannered, full-of-chuckles character he portrays on the air? Or is he actually a rogue, an outlandish ogre, the sort of fellow who might, for instance, break a golf club over his caddie's head in a fit of rage?

Whatever might prompt such a question, you might ask. Or, who cares? Well, at least one reader cares. He signs his name, simply, "Pete," and he sent me the following letter in an envelope bearing a Glenview, Ill., postmark:

"Dear Mr. Rollow: On Saturday night, while broadcasting the Cubs game, Jack Brickhouse mentioned that after reading the first round scores of the Westchester Golf Classic he felt like throwing his own clubs away. I would suggest he do so. Having caddied for him a few times I know that on a golf course he isn't the nice guy he appears to be on TV.

"I heard from another caddie about one time when he was having an even worse game than usual. He approached a medium-length par 3 that had a house with a fence around the yard behind the green.

"Mr. Brickhouse pulled out a wood while his caddie insisted he only needed an iron. However, Jack was sure he had made the right selection. Upon hitting the ball, the caddie could be heard saying 'look out, that ball's pretty well hit—back, back, back, hey-hey,' as the ball landed in the yard over the fence.

"Mr. Brickhouse immediately fired the caddie."

Well!, as another Jack, by the name of Benny, would say. Say it ain't so, Jack.

"Okay, I WILL say it ain't so," said Jack Brickhouse when I called him to get his side of the story. "This is an old rap," Brickhouse said with a laugh. "I hear that story all the time, about how I fired a caddie for yelling 'hey-hey.' Somebody yells that almost every time I step up to the tee.

"I never fired a caddie in my life. I was a caddie myself for six years. It's the greatest thing a young kid can do. I took a group of 75 North Shore caddies out to Wrigley Field to see the Cubs just a couple of weeks ago. And don't forget that as a director of the Western Golf Association I am very interested in arranging scholarships for deserving caddies."

With the caddie subject disposed of, Brickhouse launched into a discussion of putters. He admitted that, although he does not abuse caddies, he tends to get pretty angry on the green.

"I don't throw putters," Jack said, "but I do bawl them out pretty much. They have a tendency to want to get even with me. I am convinced that if you opened up a putter, you would find a brain, a heart and a nervous system inside.

"Every once in a while I find a putter that got up on the wrong side of the bed that day and takes it out on me. This, I admit, makes me mad. But I guess the fellows who manufacture golf shafts have to make a living, too. They have to make putters a little temperamental."

John Husar, Cooper's associate at the *Tribune*, put it this way:

They say that when Jack Brickhouse finishes a round of golf at North Shore, an assistant pro looks up expectantly and Brick mumbles something like "a 3-iron, 7-iron, my wooden-shafted putter and my 3-wood."

That's all he needs to say. The assistant goes into a stockroom where duplicates of Brickhouse's clubs are kept for emergency replacement purposes.

Brickhouse takes his golf seriously, you see – befitting one who last week was made an honorary director of the Chicago District Golf Association.

Usually, these awards are made for something more than breaking 115, and so Brick publicly – and no doubt properly – has vowed to shoulder the "magnificent responsibility of going out and earning it."

What this may mean, however, is simply altering his magnificent style on the links —for the good of golf, of course. His golf image always has concerned him, as he attested by bringing a couple of long-time pals to his black-tie installation with the explanation: "I wanted these guys to see with their own eyes what a great humanitarian, sportsman, civic booster, and all-around fine gentleman they have been obscenely calling a thief all these years."

But Howard J. Johnson and Niles Swanson quietly shook their heads. They knew, as we soon shall see, just how that big, friendly Brickhouse really performs when he trades his Cubs' or Bears' microphone for a golf club.

Three years ago at Ridgemoor, Big Jack stormed thru a formal book review in the clubhouse to hit a shot off a balcony.

"It's out of bounds," Johnson had said when the high hook bounced onto the porch. "Show me the stakes," Brickhouse replied, knowing full well that the white stakes had been stored for the winter.

So Brickhouse and his caddie (and Johnson and heaven knows how many others) clattered up the stairs and thru a main lounge where some 125 women were raptly listening to a book review by a prominent socialite. Without batting an eye, Brickhouse stomped up the aisle, rattled open a balcony door, and went out to hit his shot, the women gathering at the windows.

"The darn thing was, he actually got it

thru the iron railing and close enough to the green to save his par," grumbled Johnson. Then Brick tipped his hat and clattered back thru the room, signing autographs and further devastating the book review.

When he is losing, Brickhouse habitually doubles and quadruples bets on the 18th tee — which can lead to interesting outbursts. "He does this all the time, always thinking he's going to win," Johnson said. "He's spent a fortune this way." Once he wound up playing a par-3 final hole five times, losing every time, until he finally drove his ball into the crotch of a tree. "You should have seen the tree," attested Johnson.

Brickhouse's high point came at North Shore a year ago when, after improving all bets, he proceeded to drive his ball into the setting sun. No one saw it, but Brick finally determined it must have landed on the roof of an old pumphouse beside the fairway.

Naturally, he wouldn't think of taking a penalty and playing the shot again. Brickhouse sent the caddies for a ladder.

"Eight or 10 foursomes played thru," Johnson said, "and when the caddies finally came back they had the oldest, creakiest, most worn out ladder you've ever seen."

Brickhouse, who weighs about 210, climbed high enough to see at least a hundred abandoned balls on the roof. Even so, he insisted on trying to find his own Spalding when the ladder suddenly broke.

There he was, dangling in 15 feet of space,

his arms around a parapet. Swanson hurriedly rearranged what was left of the ladder and got as high as four rungs. Still there were six inches between his shoulders and Brickhouse's kicking feet.

"Okay, Jack, let go," Swanson said just as Ray Bennigsen, the old Chicago Cardinal president, was nudging Johnson and saying: "Look at Jack's spikes."

Sure enough, Jack let go and, when his golf spikes dug into Swanson's shoulders, both shrieked as Swanson leaped, flipping both into Olympic back dives.

Johnson swears that Brickhouse was knocked out and still got up eventually to stalk back to the tee and try again, this time with his penalty. Then he knocked one out of bounds.

"He came back up the fairway on the right side and every 20 yards he'd smack a club against a tree. When he got to the green he didn't even have a putter," Johnson recalled.

Ah, yes, it was another big day at the cash register in the pro shop.

Thank you, Cooper. Thank you, John. At least you could have changed the names to protect the innocent!

I was only eight years old when Red Grange of Illinois ran wild against Michigan in the dedication game at Memorial Stadium in Champaign on October 18, 1924.

So it was a real kick to sit on the dais with the Galloping Ghost 50 years later and participate in the Red Grange Golden Anniversary banquet at the Ramada Inn in Champaign. A full house was on hand to commemorate the most-talked-about individual performance in collegiate football history.

In the weeks preceding the testimonial, I had worked on a WGN Television documentary entitled "Red Grange: 12 Minutes to Immortality." WCIA in Champaign received permission to air our show the night of the dinner.

The printed banquet program, as prepared by Tab Bennett and his staff in the university's sports information office, contained two memorable quotations, one from Grantland Rice, the other from Grange's coach at Illinois, Bob Zuppke.

Grantland Rice had written as follows:
"A streak of fire, a breath of flame,
Eluding all who reach and clutch,
A gray ghost thrown into the game
That rival hands may never touch;
A rubber bounding, blasting soul,
Whose destination is the goal—
Red Grange of Illinois."

And Zuppke had put it this way in 1936:
"Grange was a genius of motion. I saw that and made a team picture with him at the focal point. He ran with no waste motion . . . I once made a trip to the Kaibab Forest on the edge of the north rim of the Grand Canyon and as a deer ran out onto the grass plains, I said: 'There goes Red Grange!'

The freedom of movement was so similar to Red's."

My remarks at the Grange dinner included the Damon Runyon line that "Red Grange was three or four men and a horse rolled into one. He was Jack Dempsey and Babe Ruth and Al Jolson and Paavo Nurmi and Man O'War."

I noted that Quin Ryan had broadcast the Illinois-Michigan game on WGN Radio in 1924, the year the station went on the air. A listener called WGN after Grange had scored four touchdowns in less than 12 minutes and suggested the station get another sports announcer. "The one you have obviously doesn't know a touchdown from a first down," the caller complained. "No man can score that many touchdowns in that short a time!"

I said it was comforting to join a winner like Grange following a broadcasting year in which the Cubs blew it, the White Sox blew it, the Bears blew it, the Bulls blew it and the Hawks blew it. "In fact," I added, "I called dial-a-prayer and they hung up on me."

George Halas of the Bears was there to honor Grange and he laid it on the line: "Red Grange had more impact on football than any man in this century. And even though there are 26 years left in this century, my statement will still stand up when the hundred years have passed."

Ray Eliot, the former Illinois coach, took note of the #77 jersey Grange made famous: "It's virtually impossible to throw two 7s at the same time!"

And before bringing on Grange, Eliot said candidly: "How do you introduce a ghost?"

I recall a number of things Red Grange spoke about that night.

He dwelled on Zuppke at length. He said Zup once described one of his players as having deceptive speed: "He's slower than he looks!"

He said Zup once complained his prospects for the coming season were lousy because "I haven't lost any of my players."

He said Zup once told a reporter Grange wore #77 simply because "he stood behind the guy wearing #76 and in front of the guy wearing #78!"

He said the closest Zup ever came to using profanity was to call a player a "lemon" or a "jackass." Red added: "If he called you that, it meant that in his book you were zero zero zero."

He told about the student who consulted his teacher about the significance of the one D and three F's he had gotten on his report card. "It means," analyzed the teacher, "that you're concentrating too much on one subject."

Grange acknowledged a telegram from President Gerald R. Ford, the ex-Wolverine football player. "When I assumed my present office," the wire read, "I never dreamed that I'd be congratulating someone who kicked the heck out of Michigan."

Red Grange, football immortal. It had been a night to remember.

And earlier in the day, they had held a press conference to herald his return to the campus. Grange told of meeting Babe Ruth one day in New York and getting two pieces of advice. "Kid," the

Bambino warned, "don't believe a damn thing they write about you and don't pick up too many checks!"

With his typical modesty, Grange refused to take credit for making pro football the game it is today. "That," laughed Red Grange, "is like saying the Johnstown flood was caused by a leaky toilet in Altoona."

X

On the Lighter Side

Some of my days as Cubs' telecaster seemed much longer than others. One such afternoon was May 24, 1974. The Cubs and St. Louis were scoreless in the top of the ninth at Wrigley Field.

For the Cubs, it was Rick Reuschel pitching, Tom Lundstedt catching, Billy Williams at first and Matt Alexander, a real speed merchant, at third.

The Cardinals got runners on first and third with one out and sent up Tim McCarver to pinch-hit. McCarver grounded to Williams wide of first. Reuschel ran to cover first in case Williams decided to go for two by way of second.

Williams rightly figured there wasn't time for a double play. He fired the ball home to catcher Lundstedt. Ted Simmons, the runner on third, was now trapped between third and home. Lundstedt chased Simmons back toward third and then threw to third baseman Alexander. Simmons turned around and headed for home again, Alexander in hot pursuit.

Alexander wanted to throw. One problem: no one covering home. Simmons reached the plate well in front of Alexander's clutching hand.

Final: Cardinals 1, Cubs 0.

Cubs' manager Whitey Lockman's classic line afterwards: "At least we had our fastest man chasing him across home plate!"

Russ Meyer, The Mad Monk, was one of the most unforgettable characters I've met in sports.

He started his big league pitching career with the Cubs and later distinguished himself with the Phillies and Dodgers. The Cubs eventually got him back again if for no other reason than the fact they rarely could beat him once he left Chicago. In fact, Russ beat the Cubs 24 times in 27 decisions!

The incident which sold me on the Mad Monk's claim to immortality happened in between his stints with the Cubs. The game involved Philadelphia and Brooklyn. I wasn't there, and I regret I wasn't, but the way Meyer recalled it for me later, he was pitching this day and his temper had gotten the better of him. Umpire Augie Donatelli kicked him out of the game.

Infuriated, The Mad Monk picked up his resin bag and flung it high into the air. As he stomped off toward the dugout, the resin bag came down and plopped him right on top the head, immersing his face in dust.

It was a pinpoint bombing job at its best.

In 1972, at Three Rivers Stadium in Pittsburgh, the Pirates had runners on first and second, nobody out, Manny Sanguillen at bat. That's nothing new. For years it seems the Pirates have had two on and none out against the Cubs.

But this day, I announced: "Here's where the

Cubs get their first triple play of the season. I know it sounds like the impossible dream but the impossible dream is very much a part of baseball. Part of baseball's glamor is its unpredictability."

No sooner had the words left my mouth than Sanguillen slugged a hard ground ball to Ron Santo. He stepped on third, fired to Glenn Beckert at second, Beckert relayed to Joe Pepitone at first. Triple play!

The other side of it in Pittsburgh was the night the Cubs carried a 2-1 lead into the bottom of the ninth, Fergie Jenkins pitching. "All right, the Cubs have a tissue-paper lead," I announced, and then said assuredly, "and there's no one I'd rather have pitching for me in a spot like this than Ferguson Arthur Jenkins."

A quick single then brought up Roberto Clemente, who swung in that patented Clemente manner and the most I could say as the ball arched over the wall was "Oh, brother . . . ."

Veterans Stadium, Philadelphia. Willie Montanez batting for the Phillies, bases loaded, Jim Todd pitching for the Cubs.

"Lots of great pitchers have been in this kind of jam over the years," I commented, "and they proved their greatness by escaping without further trouble."

Came the pitch. Came the grand-slam home run.

It was July 5, 1974, when the Atlanta Braves showed up at Wrigley Field to launch a four-game series with a Friday doubleheader. The Cubs won Game 1, 4-1. The second game was tied, 2-2, in the bottom of the ninth.

As Andy Thornton picked up a bat to lead off for the Cubs, I made this point: "Even though both of these teams have respected power, not a single home run has been hit here today. The wind has been a slight deterrent. But the day isn't over yet."

Max Leon threw the first pitch of the inning and Thornton hit it out. Cubs 3, Braves 2.

That series, incidentally, marked the final appearance in Wrigley Field for Henry Aaron as an active player. He got repeated standing ovations and this outward adulation gave me a spine-tingling thrill just to be there.

Aaron rewarded the fans. He hit number 725 off Rick Reuschel, who survived it to win, 4-3, in the series finale. It was Aaron's 50th career homer at Wrigley Field. I covered all 50. Jeepers.

We were in Minnesota for a Sox-Twins night telecast. The Sox had lost. Now director Jack Jacobson and I were making that mad dash for the airport. We got there just in time but they didn't have two seats together and I was anxious to recoup the gin rummy losses I had incurred en route to the Twin Cities.

"You take that single," I told Jake, "and I'll take that other single in the back and try to talk that guy into changing seats with you."

So I sat down beside this pleasant-looking gentleman and introduced myself. "I'm Jack Brick-house, the Sox broadcaster. The Twins whacked us tonight and not only that, I'm way behind in the gin game. Would you mind switching seats with my buddy so we can finish our game?"

"Not at all, Mr. Brickhouse," he said, graciously. With that, he rose, very carefully, and only then did I notice he had only one leg. I was mortified but didn't want to embarrass the man by calling him back. As he trudged slowly down the aisle, I could see Jake slinking in his seat. He wasn't anxious to let the other passengers know he was a friend of mine!

It was 1974 and Pat Pieper, the public address voice of the Cubs, sauntered into the clubhouse at Wrigley Field to get the line-up. He was 88 years old at this point, with 71 years of service to the Cubs dating back to the megaphone days.

I always had the inner feeling that it would be illegal to start a Cubs' home game without Pat's crisp tones first commanding the fans to "have your pencils and scorecards ready and I will give you the correct line-ups for today's game. The batteries . . . ."

When Pat arrived on this particular day, outfielder Jerry Morales and one or two of his associates were talking about shoes.

"Let me tell you something," the venerable Pieper intoned. "You see these shoes I'm wearing? They're French Shriners, and I've worn them to Wrigley Field since 1937. I get them repaired every couple of years. They've held up tremendously well and they're comfortable, so I've had no reason to change shoes in 37 years."

Said a nearby reporter: "What about your socks, Pat?"

Pat Pieper, a remarkable man, took the joke with a grain of salt and continued about his rounds.

Jim Gallagher gained fame as the Cubs' front office boss in 1945 when he swung the deal with the Yankees for Hank Borowy. "I broke into a cold sweat after the transaction," Jim told me later. "I suddenly realized that I was making about $10,000 a year—but I had just shelled out $90,000 of somebody else's money!" Borowy, though, went on to pitch the Cubs to the pennant.

I was kibitzing a gin rummy game some time later at Gallagher's apartment. Jim was going head-and-head with Dave Rush, the Western Union man. Gallagher owned a parakeet, and the bird perched on his hand and kept pecking at the seven of spades. Jim figured the parakeet must know something— and discarded it.

"Gin," yelled Rush.

Gallagher grabbed the bird, put him in his cage, pulled the cover down and wouldn't talk to him for two days!

There I was broadcasting Mayor Daley's Prep Bowl, the football classic, late in 1957. "Ladies and gentlemen," I reported, "there is time for only one more play and Mendel Catholic and Calumet have battled to a scoreless tie. You simply couldn't ask for a more appropriate score because neither of these great high school teams deserves to lose here at Soldier Field on the lakefront. Mendel Catholic has the ball on the Calumet 41-yard line and it's just about all over . . . ."

With that, Jim Brennan passed to Jim Gallagher for a 41-yard touchdown and Mendel was a last-second winner, 6-0. You might know it—I was invited to Mendel Catholic's banquet and they replayed the tape of my expert analysis as my red face got redder!

And in 1973, the Bears led the Minnesota Vikings, 10-3, with time running out in the first half at Soldier Field. The Vikings had the ball in their own territory. I nudged my color man, Irv Kupcinet, and blared: "Kup, old boy, it's comforting to know that even if something catastrophic happens the worst the Bears can have at halftime against these powerful Vikings is a 10-10 tie. That's the worst."

Seconds later, Fran Tarkenton had passed his Vikings into the end zone for a touchdown, the Bears fumbled the ensuing kickoff and on the last play of the half Fred Cox kicked a field goal. It was 13-10 Minnesota and the Vikings never were headed. Me and my big mouth.

Many sports figures long ago discovered the value of the media and the lasting impact it can have on their careers. And also on their wallets.

Don Hutson, the great Green Bay end, was an example of a player who knew somebody was always listening.

In the early 1940s, I was broadcasting a radio show on the eve of a Bears-Packers game. My guests were Curly Lambeau, the Green Bay coach, and Hutson.

There wasn't anything unusual about the interview until Hutson announced he planned to retire after the season.

Lambeau almost fainted.

Meanwhile, I was thinking I had a great scoop.

Unfortunately, it turned out to be one of a half dozen Hutson "retirements."

A few years later, I asked Hutson why he pulled those phony retirement stories. He told me it was the only way he could get more money from the Packers.

"The Packers gave me a $25 per game raise after I announced my retirement on your show," he told me.

He said it worked time and again.

In 1945 somebody could finally claim the story. After 10 years and a Hall of Fame career, Hutson retired.

Arlington Park Race Track. You know the old story. That's where the windows clean *you*. Jack Rosenberg, Arne Harris and I poured over The Racing Form. There was a variable: Arne understands The Racing Form. Rosey and I don't. Arne believes in improving the breed and he can quote past performances and those other foreign facts with authority.

It was the third race and Rosenberg had a strong hunch. The number 6 horse, a 7-to-1 shot.

Said Arne: "No chance. I've watched that horse for weeks. He gets out, then he folds."

Rosey took Arne at his word. He switched to Number 8.

Now the race was off and Number 6 broke out fast. He pulled in front by three lengths. Then it was four. Then five. And as he crossed the finish line, seven lengths in front, there was Arne yelling: "Yippee. I got him!" And he flashed a $10 win ticket on Number 6.

The last I can recall, Rosey was chasing Arne down the escalator, two steps at a time, shouting invectives in Yiddish along the way.

In Montreal, the Cubs had outlasted the Expos in a drawn-out day game and we all took off for the harness races. Lou Boudreau, Vince Lloyd, Lloyd Pettit and a handful of others. Unbeknown to us, Glenn Beckert had planned to go, changed his mind but asked Boudreau to bet his number — 1-8 — in the daily double — and turn it around, too — 8-1.

The cabbie got loused up in traffic and we arrived almost at post-time. Number 8 won the first and paid $75 to win. Boudreau looked at us and moaned: "I hope to hell the Number 1 horse loses in the second. Beckert gave me two doubles and I forgot to put 'em down."

The second race was a photo. The winner was Number 1, an 8-to-1 outsider. The daily double was worth $1,200, largest payoff in Canada in three years.

Boudreau was crestfallen. Now he started calling Beckert's room at the Queen Elizabeth after every race. He didn't want Glenn to pick up a late newspaper and think he had won $1,200. But Beckert had gone to a movie.

Later that night, when we returned to the hotel, Beckert got the word on the mix-up. I'll say this: he was a real gentleman about it, considering the amount of money involved.

Next morning, as we entered the bus to go to Jarry Park, Leo Durocher, as usual, was sitting in the first seat. I confess I never had the slightest idea how Leo would manage in a given situation but the one predictable thing he did was to commandeer that first seat on the bus.

As Boudreau got on, Durocher screeched: "Boudreau, you bleep. If you ever try to screw me out of $1,200 like you did Beckert, I'll call WGN and have your wages garnisheed."

I recall with fondness my friendship with the late Frank Darling. He was president of Local #1031 of the I.B.E.W. One of his pleasures was to accompany our crew on an occasional football trip and serve as "unofficial floating coordinator."

Frank had a bodyguard he called Captain. Captain had taken a liking to a Stetson hat worn by an acquaintance. Frank decided to buy him a gift.

Captain wore size 7. Frank went to a downtown store and paid $20 for a Stetson, size 7.

But for another $40 he bought two more Stetsons, same style, one a size 6¾, the other 7¼.

He had the store put a size 7 label in both.

Frank gave the size 7 to Captain. On the sly, he handed the other two hats to the bartender at a West Side taproom where they ate lunch almost daily.

Captain came in that first day wearing his new Stetson, proudly. He carefully placed it on the hat rack.

While Captain had lunch with Frank, the bartender watched for an opening and switched hats. He hung up the 6¾. Captain finished lunch and grabbed his hat. He felt like a pinhead. Yet, this had to be his hat. The size was marked clearly and it even had his initials in it.

Next day, the switch again. This time to the 7¼. Captain came out after lunch, the hat practically covered his eyes. He began to worry about head shrinkage.

The practical joke continued for a week until one day Captain caught the bartender in the act—and threatened to have him jailed for life!

My counterpart in Pittsburgh, the late Bob Prince, told me of a bizarre incident in his telecast of the 1960 World Series. He was teamed with Mel Allen and now it was Game 7, Pirates vs. Yankees, Forbes Field.

NBC told Prince to leave the booth after the eighth inning and head for the Pittsburgh clubhouse to conduct post-game interviews. The Pirates led at this point, 9-7, thanks in the main to Hal Smith's home run.

By the time Bob reached the dressing room, the Yanks had tied it up, 9-all, with two runs in the top of the ninth. Now they instructed him to run back up to the booth, high atop the stands, in the event of extra innings.

Even as he scrambled through the mammoth crowd once again, Prince heard that familiar and unmistakable roar. He knew the game was over, he knew Pittsburgh had won—but he had no idea who had hit the home run.

What Prince did know was that he was in danger of being late. He had to return to that clubhouse in all haste. He fought around the mob and got there just in time to have an assistant director ram a microphone into his hand and tell him to start interviewing.

Prince grabbed the nearest available player, Bill Mazeroski, and asked, breathlessly: "Maz, how does it feel to be a member of a world championship team?"

"Great!" laughed Mazeroski.

That terminated the five-second interview. Prince patted Maz on the butt and went on to talk to the other players on national television.

It wasn't until he had gotten off the air that Prince learned it was Bill Mazeroski who had slammed one of the most-talked-about homers in baseball history.

Actually, I have come to believe any story involving Bob Prince, whose ability as a broadcaster was surpassed only by his phenomenal reputation as a swimmer.

On this day, he was occupying a third-floor suite overlooking the pool at the Chase Hotel in St. Louis. It was 90 feet to the water, with a seven-foot concrete deck between poolside and the building.

Pirates' first baseman Dick Stuart offered to bet Prince $20 he couldn't dive from that third-floor window into the pool.

Prince accepted the wager.

The mere fact I'm telling this story is proof that Prince made the dive successfully. He was stone sober, too.

The hotel management immediately put through an order that henceforth, Bob Prince never was to be assigned a room overlooking the pool.

Not only that, but Prince claimed Stuart never paid him the twenty bucks!

Along with talent and entertainment, commercials are the lifeblood of the broadcasting industry. There is no such thing as a corporate giant who doesn't advertise. A company that grew into a giant is Morrie Mages Sporting Goods.

Morrie Mages is to sporting goods what Ray Kroc was to hamburgers.

During the 1950s, Morrie and I started doing commercials on late night television.

On our first commercial we introduced a feature called "Mages Moment of Madness." The item featured was underpriced to encourage shoppers to stop by the store.

In the middle of the commercial I broke away from the script and said, "Morrie, are you going crazy selling this item so cheaply?"

It caught Morrie completely by surprise. All he could do was lapse into his Maxwell Street dialect and he said, "I'm witch you."

The line drew a big laugh. We decided to leave it in the commercial. The line caught on publicly and Morrie probably peddled a million "I'm Witch U" buttons.

The Mages family business boomed. They went from five stores to 14 and became one of the foremost sporting goods dealers in America.

In the early days of television there was no such luxury as videotape or delay buttons or retakes. The announcer had one take and one shot at perfection.

With those limits it wasn't any wonder there were thousands of hilarious experiences that developed from one-take sessions—especially commercials.

I did a commercial for Coral Stone. It was a siding material guaranteed to protect a home from sun, rain, hail and other forms of inclement weather. It was also very easy to clean.

I demonstrated how easy on one commercial. I took a wet cloth and tried to wipe the siding clean of crayon marks.

"Notice how easy the crayon marks are removed with a damp cloth," I said, as I started to wipe the cloth down the siding. To everyone's surprise, the cloth was covered with a gritty abrasive that could have peeled the side of a battleship. The noise was excruciating.

Another moment occurred when the company wanted me to demonstrate the durability of the product by having me hold a blow torch next to the siding. It wasn't one of my favorite assignments.

After the first commercial, I was told to hold the torch as close to the siding as possible. I followed the directions.

The next time I did the commercial I had the blue flame very close to the siding. I was reading the cue cards and not paying particular attention to the flame.

Suddenly, through the corner of my eye, I saw a black spot appear on the studio monitor. I looked at the siding and noticed a huge hole burning through the siding.

I quickly pulled the torch away and frantically searched for the correct words.

I said, "Ladies and gentlemen, I was instructed to hold this blow torch on this spot until it burned through the siding. As you noticed, it took a couple of minutes to burn a hole in the siding. That is the equivalent of a bright sun bearing down on your home for 100 years. That gives you an idea just how unbelievably durable Coral Stone really is."

I will say this for Norm Stone, the Coral Stone owner. He watched at home through tears in his eyes. He loved it.

XI
The Mailbox

Thousands of pieces of mail cross my desk at WGN each year. I get beefs, compliments, jokes, poems, inquiries and whatever. Some are caustic, some funny, some clever, some pathetic, some informative. For a long time now, I have maintained a file marked "unusual letters." It contains not only the exceptional office mail but also stacks of uncommon notes sent up to our television booths at Wrigley Field and Comiskey Park during my play-by-play days.

I originally got the idea for such a file during my early broadcasting days in Peoria. I was filling in as the announcer on a show called "Pet Corner" at WMBD when a man sent me the following letter:

Dear Mr. Brickhouse,

Please, please help us find our dog, Rachel. I actually fear for my 9-year-old daughter's sanity if this dog isn't found. Rachel is a beautiful white terrier with a brown mark on her right foreleg. She's friendly, loving and smart. She's a member of our family. We've never had anything affect us this deeply. I implore

you, Mr. Brickhouse, please help us find
Rachel.

Sincerely,

J.W. Ward

P.S. Never mind. The dog just came home.

Once I read the P.S., I figured the letter was
a gag. All of us at the station laughed about it. But
as I grew older, and started becoming exposed to
voluminous amounts of mail in Chicago, I grad-
ually realized that Mr. Ward's note hadn't been
a gag at all. Instead, as I analyzed it, he felt he
had done such a great job of composing his dramatic letter that it seemed a shame not to mail it.
To him, it wasn't simply a letter but pure literature,
chiseled out of granite, hammered out of iron.

The following letters and notes are examples
from my "unusual letter" file, with misspellings
left in, names left out and in some cases the contents shortened:

Mr. Brickhouse:

We would NEVER know who was broadcasting on WGN-TV baseball if you didn't
mention your name 10 times today during the
first game and again when you interviewed
Cochrane between games. You don't have to
be stuck on yourself or be a swell-head, you
swell-head.

Mr. Jack Brickhouse:

How can you brazenly advertise beer on
television. Do you have teen-age sons or

daughters? Would you like to see them sitting on bar stools with legs crossed, guzzling the stuff you sell? Would you like to see your wife leaning over the ironing board in a half-stupor when you come home? For the few dollars you get, you are willing to send more people down skid row.

Dear Mr. Brickhouse:

Would you wish my parents a happy 25th wedding anniversary? My German shepard is having puppies. Would you like one?

Mr. Brickhouse:

For three years I have suffered thru your play-by-play analysis and I find it appalling when you take it upon yourself to openly criticize the various playing techniques of both the Cubs and White Sox. At this moment I am referring to your analysis of the Cubs' baserunning in this, the second game of a double header with Milwaukee. Why don't you get out there on the basepaths and try running them yourself?

Jack Brickhouse:

I hope you'll do me this favor. Please say "hi" to my husband, son and daughter on a weekend because I'm not allowed to talk to them when the Cubs are on television.

Mr. Jack:

I heard you mention great humorists on the Brickhouse-Hubbard Show. Maybe you know this one, but Harry Hershfield, the well-known humorist, once wrote his own epitaph. It read this way: "Here lies the body of Harry Hershfield. If not, notify Ginsberg, the undertaker, at once!"

Dear Sir:

I find your alleged gift of gab and smart alec terms very disgusting. For one thing, why don't you say "strike" instead of "stee-rike" . . . ?

Dear Jack:

Up 'til now, I've always considered you a gallant, charming fellow but now you're on my list. Today, you announced it was Ladies Day and then you went on to add—with typical masculine superiority—that women love to come to the park and howl and shriek. You, sir, classed womanhood with hyenas and I demand a retraction.

Brickhouse:

Heard you make a remark on TV about the Golden Glove of Ron Santo. When I heard that, I laughed so hard I pissed in my pants.

Dear Jack:

I have always admired you. If you are interested in seeing me, or my picture, ask Joe
Pepitone. He has my picture.

Love ya.

Dear Jack:

Perhaps while the White Sox are touring
the east you could have the workmen at the
ball park install infra-red lamps on the light
towers. I think this would be a sure cure for
the alibis the Sox have been making about
their need for warm weather.

Cornball:

You are slipping. You only gave us the
line-up 37 times. Must be running out of
corny stories.

Dear Mr. Brickhouse:

I hope you won't think this letter unkind,
but I have noticed your thinning hair on television. I am a barber and have a special shampoo for growing hair. All you have to do is
measure the diameter of your bald spot and
let my product do the rest. You are one of 80
million people who suffer embarrassment unnecessarily. If you wonder why I am not a
millionaire with my shampoo, it's because I
can't get my message across to enough people. Why don't you help me help them and
you . . . ?

Dear Mr. Brickhouse:

Our quire is here today from Wilmette. If you want to hear us sing, we are in sexshun 16 by home plate. Thank you.

Dear Mr. Brickhouse:

Could you help me? A man owed my late husband a large sum of money. I understand this man has been seen at the race tracks. I would like to find him. Could you please get me a pass to Sportsman's and Hawthorne so I can go there and look for this dead beat?

Dear Jack:

Please tell me where you bought the light-colored overcoat you wore on TV during the Cubs' game last Thursday. I am a size 48 and can't find my size in any of the large stores. Please.

Dear Mr. Brickhouse:

I would like to know if an empire ever has been thrown out of a game. Please announce it on Sunday's TV.

Dear Mr. Brickhouse:

I am 6 years old. I would like to sit in the announcer booth at Cubs ball park. Plase invite me. Answer. I can read.

Dear Mr. Brickhouse:

Thank you for sending me the golf balls. They will last several years because I promise not to use them on water holes, even the horrible No. 9 on the par 3 course at Mission Hills. I would like to use them on a big course but I understand you have to be bar mitzvahed before you do.

Mr. Jack Brickhouse:

Keep your fingers crossed, any old run will win it.

Every time you say this, we lose. Why don't you keep your big mouth shut? You bring us bad luck. You are junival in your expressions. We had it in the bag in the 8th inning today and then you got silly and said to keep your fingers crossed. We lost.

To Jack:

Please announce that our softball team is here from Racine. And say good luck to our manager, who was unable to make it because of physical defects.

Dear Jack:

Would you do a favor for us women who watch the ball games? Please ask the cameraman to pick out a good-looking man once in awhile and show him instead of always just the shapely women. We enjoy a nice view on TV the same as you men do.

Dear Mr. Brickhouse:

I notice that when your partner Lloyd Pettit is announcing the Cubs lose. Fire him. He is not lucky for our team.

Dear Jack:

I run a disposal service up north. Just say that the used food expert is here at Wrigley field today with his family. My friends will know who you mean.

Dear Sir:

I understand you are having difficulty finding a manager for the Cubs. I hereby offer you a suggestion that should help both of us. I submit the name of my husband. His experience? He has been managing the Cubs for at least 15 years, without salary or publicity, and right here at home. I feel it is about time he received some of both and about time, too, that the Cubs received some of the valuable advice that is being wasted on me.

Perhaps you feel that you need a more experienced man, so I ask you what you have to show for the big names you have had so far?

What do you have to lose? I think you have a lot to gain, and so do I. One more summer of being chewed out for all the mistakes the Cubs make is gonna kill me.

I am so sold on my product that I offer him to you on a 10-day trial free. Whenever you start training in Bermuda, or some such nice warm climate, please remember my offer.

Dear Jack:

   I like watching the Cubs in action, especially Jose Cardenal. He's the best-looking Cub, then comes Jim Hickman, then comes you. I think you are very handsome. Bald is beautiful.

Dear Mr. Brickhouse:

   Last night I saw Randy Hundley on 10th Inning. He said that he could not squat all the way. Inclosed is a drawing on how he can get back in the line-up sooner. He can try it. It can be done before and after batting practice. It would be best if he could lay on a table.

Dear Sirs:

   My husband is an avid Cubs fan. He has been missing from home for two months. Please announce on TV that he should call me at the below-listed number for the sake of the kids and me. Thank you.

Dear Jack:

   If you read my poem on the air, please watch out for the last line.
 The Cubs will shine in '69,
 But Ernie's rhyme was the same old line.

"Bring on the Mets," we heard them say
They wish they'd never seen that day.
While those who hit were having fits
Leo said, "Who wants a Slits?"
Next year the Cubs will do their bit
But all it will be is the same old thing.

Mr. Jack Brickhouse:
    I am in the House of Correction and have been sent here for failure to give bond amounting to $200, cash or check. Will you please come and bail me out as soon as possible and oblige? I am a Cubs fan and watch you on the TV.

Dear Brick:
    You ask how old baseball is. It's as old as the Bible. It's mentioned in the first line: In the big inning. . . .

Dear Sir:
    I've enjoyed your excellent reporting of the Chicago home games for quite a number of years. I'd like to interest you in a business deal that would be very profitable to both of us. I have completed a project which I think will win me the Nobel Prize and other honors. I'll be a very wealthy man if I can get to certain European capitols. If you can invest $6,000 for my European trip, it will bring you very good interest within three months. Please advise.

Dear Jack:

I'm sorry to say but I have no comments to make on sports at this time.

Dear Jack:

Many years ago, you interviewed my father on your Man on the Street program on Channel 9. Since then, my father has considered himself a successful TV personality. He recalls the interview time and again and with much happiness.

Jack Brickhouse:

I'm standing at the press gate with 2,700 Boy Scouts. I would like to know if you can get us in.

Dear Jack:

Just for the record, the company for which I worked in 1941 received an order for a complete system of lighting for Wrigley Field, based on permanent stationary towers.

The floodlights had been shipped, with the cable, transformers, switchgear, etc., on order, when Pearl Harbor Day came along. Subsequently, a phone call came from a spokesman for Mr. Wrigley to cancel the entire order. Let me say at this point that Mr. Wrigley had been very fair with us and I can appreciate his feeling of patriotism. He suggested that we reship the floodlights to shipyards or places that would best meet or help the war effort.

This is just a brief history of the lighting of Wrigley Field, which came to an abrupt and unfortunate ending.

Dear Jack:

Just before the game, when you read the line-up, please slow down because I have trouble keeping up.

Dear Brickhouse:

I watch you on TV and look at your long wavy hair. I wonder, how do you get such a good straight part in your hair with so little material to work with?

Hey, Jack:

Get me on your camara. I'm the one with the tennis shoes in the grandstands.

Dear Mr. Ward Quaal:

Please note the following unethical procedure which your employee, Jack Brickhouse, has taken the liberty of doing publicly on television on Sept. 24, 1960. He interviewed Ernie Broglio of the Cardinals after the game and asked Broglio to publicly announce how every Pittsburgh Pirates' player should be pitched to in the World Series. He asked whether each

Pirate should be pitched high, low, inside or outside. It was an exploitation by Brickhouse and then, at the end of the interview, Jack said: "My good friend Mayo Smith, who scouts for the New York Yankees, is watching this program and I know he will be pleased to get all this valuable information."

Mr. Quaal, when a TV announcer becomes so brash and divulges such sacred information publicly, and exploits a ballplayer in so doing, I think the situation warrants some form of reprimand or even an investigation of the announcer, namely Jack Brickhouse.

The integrity of the national pastime should not be endangered because of such procedures. As you know, large amounts of money are wagered on the World Series. Such frowned upon maneuvers by Brickhouse cheapens your sports department. Please investigate the matter.

Dear Sir:

I am a patient at a state hospital in a section where we are not allowed to have our own razors. I want to buy one of those World Series books they're advertising on TV but I can't get one without buying the razor as well. Can you help me? I am a great Cubs fan, win or lose.

Dear Mr. Brickhouse:

My girl friend and I are both young, attractive and unattached. We would like to know how to meet two Chicago Bears who are equally young, attractive and unattached. Object: throwing a few passes! However, Mr. Brickhouse, it's about as easy to meet the Chicago Bears as it is to defeat the N.Y. Mets.

If no Bears are available, a few, good ol' Chicago Cubs would do nicely. Hey hey!

Dear Mr. Brickhouse:

My son is in prison and he comes up before the parole board in February. He is a real good ballplayer. Can you give me the names of some people I can write at the ballclubs so that maybe he can get a job with one of them? I thank you very much.

Hey Brickhouse:

I have a cane and it does the work of a whammy stick. Every time I touch it the Cubs lose. It worked real good last year.

Dear Jack:

Please say "hi" to Ronny. He got sick last night and couldn't come to the game today. Please say it before 2:30 because he is going to the doctor. You're great.

Dear Mr. Brickhouse:

I am 9 years old. I am in the 4th grade. I would like to ask you to give my name to

Santa Claus. I am a good baseball player but I need a baseball glove and my daddy cannot afford to buy me one. God bless you.

Mr. Jack Brickhouse:
You have a visitor at the press gate. Please let him in. He is a big fan of yours.

Dear Mr. Brickhouse:
Why did Billy Williams go to jail? The answer: because he stold second base.

Dear Mr. Brickhouse:
My daughter is a Cubs fan. The other night, when the Cubs scored two runs toward the end of the Cincinnati game, she got so excited she jumped out of her chair, fell down and broke her arm. She was wearing a Cubs pajama top, the pullover kind, at the time and we can't get it off without cutting it. She refuses to allow her Cubs shirt to be cut. Can you send her a message of cheer over the air?

Dear Jack,
Can you get me the names and addresses of all the handsome ballplayers in the Cubs' farm system who are bachelors and show promise of some day becoming major league prospects? My dream has always been to marry a major league player. I hope you can

make my dream come true. Please send the names of the basketball players, too.

Dear Mr. Jack:

Thought I would write and tell you that we watch all the Cubs games. Not that we are Cub fans. On the contrary, you have taken care of that. We are for the opposition. Don't you realize that everyone is not a Cub fan? Why must they be crammed down our throats? It's such fun to watch them lose. Every play they make is spectacular, according to you, but other teams can do every bit as good. I have seen the Cubs make errors and you say it's one of those things, yet you will ridicule the other team for the same mistakes.

I heard you criticize the Pittsburgh ball park for poor lighting when you don't have lights at all at Wrigley Field. I love baseball but I am sick of hearing the announcers taking it for granted that we are all Cub fans.

I must admit, however, that you are indeed one of the best announcers and very intellectual.

A Dodger fan.

Dear Jack Brickhouse:

I would like to broadcast the White Sox or manage the White Sox or coach the White Sox or play for the White Sox. Some day I plan to go to a game and watch the White Sox.

Dear Mr. Jack:

I only watch Channel 9 but now my TV has gone bad. I would like for you and your staff to send me a TV set. I am enclosing my address.

Dear Mr. Brickhouse:

I have two boys who are ardent Cub fans and I am writing this letter as a result of something they said (September, 1969). I am a psychiatrist and occasionally will use hypnosis as a method of therapy. Our kids said, "You ought to hypnotize the Cubs so they'll play better." In thinking about this, I've watched the past several games and see many indications both verbally and non-verbally of a depressed team. Since depression interferes with our ability to concentrate, our ability to be full of energy, eagerness, enthusiasm, etc., it is to be expected that split-second timing, reflex activity, and fine control will be influenced. This might then explain the poor hitting, pitching and fielding I've seen of late.

This can be dealt with therapeutically in many ways. A rapid method is hypnotherapy utilizing a specific technique called the "Ego Exhilarative Technique." It certainly seems funny to me as I think of it but the Cubs do seem to need a psychiatrist at present just as much or more than they need someone to administer first aid when they are injured. I hope that by the time you read this, they are again winning ball games but if they are not, what I've mentioned is only a thought of my own which in some way expresses my wish for magic for the Cubs. If they remain in their present mood, they could finish in third or even fourth place.

Dear Sir:

I am a Cub fan for 60 years and I have never found anyone who enjoyed your broadcasting. They call you Quack Quack Brickhouse. I now listen to WMAQ on radio and watch Channel 32 television. I hope Mr. Wrigley wakes up and gets another station to broadcast the Cub games.

Dear Jack:

When Ernie Banks hit that home run in the 9th yesterday with Ron Santo on base to beat the Padres, I started yelling "hey hey" at the top of my lungs, just like you do. But the back door of my kitchen was open and three policemen showed up to see if I was all right. Seems one of my neighbors down the street thought there was something drastically wrong at my house. I was really embarrassed.

Dear Sir:

I have decided to become a Cub pitcher. It is so easy. All you have to do is throw the ball right in the middle of the catcher's glove. I was watching the Phillies pitcher yesterday.

He was pitching the ball high, low, left, right, outside, inside. But the Cub pitcher kept putting it in the same spot every time. What is wrong with these men?

Dear Mr. Brickhouse:

My older brother is the big shot on the block and just because he doesn't like the Cubs, nobody else on the block outside of me likes the Cubs, either. Could you please send me some information on how I can get even with him? His favorite team is the Cincinnati Reds.

Dear Mr. Brickhouse:

How come? If a righthanded batter is batting, how come he is on the left side of the catcher and on the same side as left field? If a lefthanded batter is batting, how come he is on the right side of the catcher and the same side as right field? How come a righthanded pitcher throws from the left side of the field and a lefthanded pitcher throws from the right side of the field? After hitting the ball, how come the runner runs to the right field side for first base when I was taught to read from left to right? So how come first base is not third base and how come third base is not first base? The batter should run to third instead of first, right or left. So how come?

Dear Mr. Brickhouse:

Is it true that Richie Scheinblum said that the best thing about playing for the Cleveland Indians is the fact that you don't have to go to Cleveland on road trips?

Jack:

I am here selibrating my birthday with 10 other people. I am naming them below. I can only think of nine.

Dear Sir:

There are about 500 ballplayers and some are supposed to be educated. When they go on your 10th Inning show, ask them if they believe in voodooism and witches riding on brooms. They must, otherwise why are they afraid to wear No. 13. They must be nuts or plain foolish. Bill Tuttle is the only player who wears No. 13. And he is alive.

Dear Mr. Brickhouse:

I have an idea to help the Cubs. They have nine pitchers so they should have each pitcher pitch one inning in each game. Hobbie could pitch the first inning and retire the first three men. Then Curtis pitches the second inning and so on. I would mix lefties with righties and their motions and styles would be different. How can I let the manager know about it?

Dear Jack Brickhouse:
I have a parakeet 1½ years old. He watches your telecasts and every time Ron Santo is batting he says "strike three." Why he picks on poor Ron I'll never know.

Dear Mr. Brickhouse:
There seems to be an argument between my mother and brother about who is the champion finger-nail biter in the major leagues. My mother says Don Hoak and my brother says Yogi Berra. Would you please settle the argument?

Mr. Brickhouse:
My 8-year-old son has watched you on television practically all of his life. We took him to a game for the first time last week. During the 7th inning, he said: "Jack Brickhouse must be sick." When we asked him why he said that, his reply was: "Because he hasn't said a word all day." Apparently, he didn't realize you are on TV only.

Dear Jack:
Of all the rotten luck. I had to be graduating when Ron Santo was on 10th Inning. When I learned of it, I was good and mad at the world except for Ron, of course. Could it possibly be arranged to have him on the air again? I collect everything of him I can, like

photos and stories. I even print his name on all of my folders. I guess it's rather silly but it can't be helped.

Jack Brickhouse:

Do you think that people can write the line-up down as fast as you give it on TV?

You should give it slow enough so people could write it down or just keep quite. You are stuppid.   .

Dear Jack:

Since your nose always looks red on our color TV, my cousin made up this song. We think you know the tune. No offense was intended:

Brickhouse the red-nosed sportsman,
Had a very shiny nose
And if you ever saw it,
You would even say it glowed.
All of the other sportsmen
Used to laugh and call him names,
They wouldn't let poor Jack
Announce any baseball games.
Then one sunny World Series game
Wrigley came to say
Brickhouse, with your nose so bright,
Won't you announce my game tonight?
Then all the sportsmen loved him
As they shouted out with glee
Brickhouse, the red-nosed sportsman
You'll go down in history.

Dear Mr. Brickhouse:

My 2-year-old son watches baseball on television because he is fascinated by the Hamm's commercial with the bears and the singing beavers. Lately, however, it seems that every time you play it he's on the potty. Could you please arrange to have it played more often?

Inasmuch as I am an only child, I always considered this letter a classic:

Dear Roy,

It has been a long time since we saw each other as children. I don't mind your never writing me but I think you should at least write our sister Mae once in awhile. I understand you're a broadcaster now and use the name Jack Brickhouse. If you have a family, here's wishing you and yours a Merry Christmas and a Happy New Year.

Your loving brother,

Edward P. A. O'Toole.

XII

The Hall of Fame

When the broadcasters' section of the Hall of Fame was originated in 1978, I hoped I'd be considered. But I never dreamed I'd be considered so soon.

I was really surprised. I'll never forget when the phone rang in January of 1983.

It was Bowie Kuhn. He said he was proud to inform me that I had just been given the Ford Frick Award and I'd be honored at the Hall of Fame Induction ceremonies that July. It took me months to fully realize what happened and it didn't really sink in until a couple of Hall of Famers paid a special little tribute.

First, I received a hand-written note from Ted Williams. It read: "I have always considered you one of my good friends and I am very happy for you. Congratulations on going into the Hall of Fame."

The second event occurred at Cooperstown. I was at a cocktail party the night before at the Otsego Hotel—the big, stately hotel that sets on the lakefront in Cooperstown. I was talking to Joe DiMaggio when a fellow asked Joe for his autograph. Joe signed and said to the man, "I'm sure

you'd like the autograph of another Hall of Famer—
Jack Brickhouse."

Right then it hit me. I thought, "I'm in the
same lodge as these guys. Wow!"

It is the greatest honor a person in my profession can receive. I still have trouble believing
it sometimes.

I heard from people all over the world. I hap-
pen to be lucky enough to belong to eight other
Hall of Fame organizations (National Sports Broad-
casters and Sport Writers in Salisbury, North
Carolina; Chicago Press Club Journalism; Bradley
University; Greater Peoria Sports Hall of Fame;
Chicago Cubs; Illinois High School Association
Coaches; American Sportscasters Association;
Greater Chicago Sports Hall of Fame). I am proud
of each and every one, but there is only one Base-
ball Hall of Fame.

On the day of the ceremony I wasn't really
nervous. All I was worried about was whether the
wind would blow my speech off the podium or
if the microphone wouldn't be working.

Jack Rosenberg wrote the speech for me. I
read it over and I wouldn't have changed a comma.
It was an absolutely perfect speech for the occasion. Jack really came through. All I had to do was
read it. And it was very well received. When people like Robin Roberts and Frank Cashen and Tom
Haller come to you afterwards and ask for copies,
you know you've done something special. Here's
the speech I gave right after Ralph Kiner and
Bowie Kuhn gave me the award:

I stand this day on what I consider the hallowed baseball ground of Cooperstown.

I feel at this moment like a man who is 60 feet 6 inches tall.

On a clear day in this quaint central New York village, you can hear and see and feel the echoes of baseball's storied past.

The atmosphere to me is breathless and humbling.

It has been my privilege to broadcast the exploits of the Chicago Cubs and the Chicago White Sox for 40 years or more. There in Wrigley Field and Comiskey Park, I have experienced the joy and the heartbreak—probably more of the latter than the former—but Chicago and its beautifully-loyal fans have had a resiliency which has kindled a perpetual flame of hope.

In the fantasy of my dreams, I have imagined myself as the announcer for a Cubs-White Sox World Series—a Series that would last 7 games, with the final game going extra innings before being suspended because of darkness at Wrigley Field.

Even as I accept this award, my life as a baseball broadcaster flashes before me. The drum beats on. The cities change. The boundaries change. The stadia change. The faces change. The announcers change. But the game remains essentially the same. Nine men on a side, three strikes and you're out. It's a contradiction, baseball is. It can be the simplest of games, yet it can be the most involved. It is the game I love.

The trains, the planes, the cabs, the buses — they have carried me millions of miles through the years to get me where I most wanted to be — the ball game. A reporter once told me that even if *I* didn't make Cooperstown, my suitcase probably would. Fortunately for me, we arrived together.

And I knew I was in the right place almost immediately. I saw a blur. That had to be Brooks Robinson going to his left. I saw a clutch base hit. That had to be George Kell. I saw a majestic high kick on the mound. That had to be Juan Marichal. I saw a quiet, firm image in the dugout. That had to be Walter Alston. I saw a typewriter, or was it a VDT? That had to be Sy Burick. For a boy from Peoria to have his name intertwined with theirs, well . . . . only in America.

It is with the deepest sincerity that I thank my company — the WGN Continental Broadcasting Company in Chicago — for believing in the entertainment value of baseball on radio and television — and for believing in me. You will pardon my pride if I insist that our call letters — WGN — are the most respected in the nation. Countless people at WGN and elsewhere have brought me to this broadcasting pinnacle today. You know who you are — and you have my undying gratitude.

Here on this memorable afternoon in Cooperstown, my heart tells me I have travelled the 90 feet from third to home and scored standing up. Thank you very much.

XIII

Extra Innings

A funny thing happened to me on the way to the 1980s. I found a formula for making a living without working. I became a sports announcer.

Recollections of my past simply are not filed chronologically in my mind, so you'll pardon if I ramble here and there. Some say I ramble on the air anyway. Why change now?

My luck has run hot and cold. I came to Chicago in 1940 and the only year I covered the White Sox exclusively was 1945. That's right, sports fans, the Cubs won the pennant in 1945.

It could be that I've broadcast enough losers to make the *Guinness Book of World Records*.

The thought has occurred to me that I'd love to have someone pull out the final standings of all the teams I've covered and simply reverse the order of finish. How sweet it would be.

"Hey-Hey"

Every now and then someone asks me how "Hey-Hey" became my trademark. Webster's *New*

World Dictionary defines the word "Hey" as being "an exclamation to get attention."

Therefore, Brickhouse's translation of "Hey-Hey" was meant to double the impact of a spontaneous celebration.

For me, it was always the natural thing to say after a Cub or a White Sox player homered.

As well-known as that phrase turned out to be, it all came about by accident.

There are times when an announcer will fall in love with a phrase or a word without realizing it.

For example, I was broadcasting a Golden Gloves boxing match in Chicago Stadium. The next day Bruce Dennis, the program manager, called me in and wanted me to listen to the tape of the broadcast.

Just five minutes into it, I told him to shut it off. Every time there was a right hand thrown in the fight I described it as "a whistling right." I had fallen in love with the word "whistling."

Apparently, I had been doing the same thing with the baseball telecasts when a Cub would homer. One day in the 1950s, Hank Sauer hit a homer for the Cubs and I looked at my monitor. The words "Hey-Hey" were filling up the screen. I had been saying it without realizing it and the crew decided to call me on it.

We decided to keep it going. It wasn't unusual for an announcer to have a certain identifiable saying like Harry Caray's "Holy Cow" or Russ Hodges' "Bye-Bye Baby."

I would have to say that "Hey-Hey" turned out to be a pretty good identification tag for me.

I've recounted some of the exciting stories I managed to get. Fairness requires that I tell about a couple that got away.

I had done hundreds of radio shows with hundreds of guests. How was I to know that this particular night would peak my curiosity about one of the touchiest issues in the history of baseball? The 1919 Black Sox Scandal.

I was polling listeners one month on the greatest Cubs and White Sox teams of all-time. It made sense to invite Buck Weaver to be on the show. Buck was the third baseman on the 1919 White Sox. Buck was elected by my listeners.

The show went fine. Afterwards, Buck and I went out for a cup of coffee.

We were making small talk when Buck turned the subject to the 1919 scandal. He told me he had one ambition and that was to clear his name.

He told me he annually applied for reinstatement and invariably the commissioner would answer that there was nothing to be done since Buck had refused to testify in the trial.

Unfortunately, people forgot the accused players didn't testify on advice from their counsel.

On this evening, Buck really intensified my interest. And here's why:

The players of that era were not protected in baseball as well as today's players. What protection could baseball guarantee these men for coming forth and telling their story?

I am not referring to the players who took the bribes. There was never a question on my part that they no longer belonged in the game.

But what about a man like Buck Weaver, who

said he was approached and refused to take part—
and that his only crime was not talking about it?

I couldn't help but think these men were playing with some rough characters. What guarantee
did they have that baseball would have given them
and their families protection? They had no guarantee baseball could or would support them.

That being the case, it is understandable why
a person like Buck would not talk even though he
was innocent of any wrong doing.

I told Buck I thought I could help clear his
name. I suggested he take a lie detector test with
only the lie detector operator, Buck and me or one
other reporter present. He could submit the two
or three questions that needed to be asked.

I promised if he passed I could guarantee him
enough publicity and enough public outcry to
force baseball to clear his name. I also promised
him if it did not come out in his favor he could
tear it up and not a word would ever be revealed.

If I had been Buck, I would have thought nothing could be better than to clear my name in this
manner. But for some reason, he turned me down.

In January of 1963, Mary Hornsby, the step-
daughter of Rogers Hornsby, called the office.
"Dad is sitting up for the first time after eye surgery," she said. "How about getting some of the
boys and visiting him at the hospital?"

Lou Boudreau, Harry Creighton, Jack Rosenberg and I quickly headed for the hospital. Rosenberg earlier had written a feature story on Hornsby
for the *Chicago Tribune*'s Sunday magazine section.

He had stuck strictly to the baseball views of the game's greatest right-handed hitter and bypassed Hornsby's personal life, omissions The Rajah appreciated.

As we all entered Hornsby's room, he looked at Rosey and said: "That was a fine story you wrote on me in the *Tribune*. Now I'm going to give you a story that will be the best magazine piece you ever wrote. I've never told it to anybody and I don't want to give you the story while anybody else is here."

Hornsby's life had been pretty much an open book and all of us were extremely curious.

"Thanks, Rog," Rosey told him. "Why don't you rest up over the weekend and I'll come back Monday so we can talk about it." Hornsby agreed.

That was a Friday afternoon.

Saturday morning, the newsroom called. Hornsby was dead.

How do you know when it's time to consider retirement? Well, I got a pretty good clue while on vacation in Spain. I was talking to an American who had been coaching basketball there. After a long conversation, he asked: "Did you say your name was Brickhouse?" I nodded. Then he said, "I remember a broadcaster in the states named Brickhouse. Was that your father?"

That Last Season

My final baseball season—1981—was marred by the baseball strike.

Yet, it was very memorable for me. Every ball club made a spontaneous gesture that never failed to warm my heart.

The last time around the league as the Cubs' television broadcaster meant two things to me—a great thrill and a real choker. It was as if I were bidding farewell to one of my best friends. In one way I was saying good-bye. And in another way, I was just saying I won't see you as much but I'll still be around.

Even the umpires gave me a little show of appreciation. They all wanted to say thanks a lot. I am proud of that because it showed me they realized what I had done all those years.

I had moments with umpires. But I was never one to stick it to them. I couldn't destroy the public's confidence in the sport. I could never find any reason to undermine an umpire.

The travel can wear down a person. After all those years it took a lot out of me. I tired of living out of a suitcase and always being away from home. I made as many 3:30 in the morning landings at airports as any person in this country. The road is no bargain.

It sounds like I'm nit-picking a little. It was difficult to get a good meal after a game and a person really can't enjoy himself during the time before a night game. I just didn't miss that aspect of the business as much as I thought I would.

But I do miss the players and the game itself. Fortunately, I've been able to stay close enough to the game that I still get out once in awhile. At the same time I can enjoy other aspects of my life.

One advantage now is if it isn't a good game I can get up and leave.

I'll borrow a line from the great Bob Hope to summarize my career in broadcasting: "It may have been a headache—but it never was a bore!" Thanks for the memories— and Thanks for Listening!

Since we're in extra innings, let's pretend that there's a rain delay and I have a chance to make a few calls of my own.

—Casey Stengel once told me he had one unfulfilled dream: to see Mickey Mantle play one full season on two good legs.

—Ted Williams had the trait of every successful professional: he was dedicated to becoming a dominant player.

—My favorite Wrigley Field baseball memory? No contest. Watching Ernie Banks hit Number 500 off Atlanta's Pat Jarvis on May 12, 1970.

—If you can name better managers than Al Lopez and Walter Alston, you'll still have to convince me.

—Nelson Fox and Luis Aparicio. They went together like State & Madison.

—When I think of Hank Sauer, I think of home runs and chewing tobacco, but not necessarily in that order.

—You can say I exaggerate, but the 10 minutes I once spent listening to Roberto Clemente discuss hitting was the equivalent of spending 10 minutes in Einstein's study.

—Billy Williams belongs in the Hall of Fame. Period.

—I defy anyone to name a better commercial announcer than the late Frank Babcock, who for years was the voice of Standard Oil on our Bears' broadcasts.

—J. C. Caroline recognized football for what it is: a bodily contact sport.

—The Game of Life would be blessed with more men like DePaul's Ray Meyer. But he is one of a kind.

—Can there be any doubt Pete Rose could make a decent buck as a media consultant?

—Bill George created the linebacking position as football knows it today. Dick Butkus revolutionized it.

—If I could turn the clock back and repeat one football broadcast, make it December 12, 1965, the day the Bears' Gale Sayers scored an incredible six touchdowns against the 49ers.

—Oh, how I long to see the great Sid Luckman throw just one more touchdown pass. Just one more, Sid.

—All these years later, I still smile when I think of my 11 years of fun on the Brickhouse-Simon and Brickhouse-Hubbard shows on WGN Radio. Ernie Simon and Eddie Hubbard—giants of our industry.

—They talk of second effort in football. When you consider fourth effort, pencil in Walter Payton.

—If I ever own a big-time station, the first talent I'll try to hire is Wally Phillips.

—I'm entitled to my opinion, so I'll go on record as saying Bears' board chairman Ed McCaskey's rendition of "Bear Down, Chicago Bears" sounds like a cross between Rudy Vallee and Placido Domingo.

I saw a ball hit over the center-field scoreboard in Wrigley Field the one and only time it has happened. Only it wasn't a baseball. It was a golf ball, and Sammy Snead slammed it over with a 2-iron during a pre-game exhibition. If I had tried it, it would have been a long foul down the left-field line.

XIV
Lists

Steve Daley of the *Chicago Tribune* wrote of me, "Jack Brickhouse has seen more bad baseball than any person, living or dead." That may or may not be true. But through it all, I tried never to lose my perspective. Sports, especially professional sports, are a form of entertainment. They offer a chance for all of us to experience vicariously the qualities of agility, speed, power and cunning. Games can be dramatic or humdrum but even at worst they are a diversion from the daily routine, an escape that people need.

The athletes themselves are human and as is true in any profession, there are some who excel and some who don't; some who give their all and some who don't; some who are stellar examples of moral character and some who aren't. Over the years I came to know hundreds and hundreds of athletes and if I were to try to parade them all by with an observation about each, this book would be endless.

Apparently, this is an era when "lists" are in vogue, so for purposes of this book the publishers gave me a list of categories and asked that I mark down the first names that came to my head. The results:

Competitors	Unforgettable Characters
Dick Butkus	Casey Stengel
Pete Rose	Jose Cardenal
Walter Payton	Russ Meyer
Mike Ditka	Dick Selma
Jerry Sloan	Jay Johnstone
Norm Van Lier	Moe Drabowsky
Bobby Hull	Satchel Paige
Rick Sutcliffe	Dizzy Dean
Tom Seaver	Bill Faul
George Connor	Frank Lane
Ron Santo	Saul Rogovin
Rogers Hornsby	Joe Pepitone
Red Grange	Dizzy Trout
Fergie Jenkins	
J. C. Caroline	
Nellie Fox	
Stan Mikita	
Ted Lyons	

All-Time Managers

Al Lopez	Joe McCarthy
Walter Alston	Sparky Anderson
Jimmy Dykes	Earl Weaver
Chuck Tanner	Tom Lasorda
Dick Williams	Whitey Herzog
Casey Stengel	Charlie Grimm
Billy Martin	Lou Boudreau

Intensity

Dick Butkus
Pete Rose
Bill George
Early Wynn
Ed O'Bradovich
Jim Piersall

Mr. Clutch

Lou Boudreau
Reggie Jackson
Bobby Thomson
George Brett
Hank Bauer
Luke Appling

Poetry in Motion

Willie Mays
Joe DiMaggio
Gale Sayers
Walter Payton
Jesse Owens
Roberto Clemente
Luis Aparicio

All-Time Owners

Phil Wrigley
George Halas
Bill Veeck
Arthur Wirtz
The Comiskeys
John Allyn

All-Time Gentlemen

Ernie Banks
Jim Hickman
Billy Williams
Vern Gagne
Sid Luckman
Ray Meyer
Alex Agase
Bob Scheffing

All-Around Best in Baseball

Willie Mays
Joe DiMaggio
Roberto Clemente

Men I'd Like On My Side

Joe Louis
Rocky Marciano
Bo Schembechler
Dallas Green
Hank Aaron
Eddie Stanky
Phil Cavarretta
Enos Slaughter
Doug Atkins
Tony Zale

Secretaries I'd Like On My Side

Kay Joyce

My Pitchers For 4-Game Sweep

Bob Gibson
Don Drysdale
Sandy Koufax
Billy Pierce

My Coach For Big Game

George Halas
Ara Parseghian
Bob Zuppke

My Hitter Long-Ball Situation

Hank Aaron	Stan Musial
Dick Allen	Ernie Banks
Ted Williams	Willie McCovey

My Teacher Hitting a Baseball	My Umpire For Big Game
Lew Fonseca	Jocko Conlan

One Player I Want Back	My Favorite Gin Rummy Player
Lou Brock	Jack Brickhouse

All-Time Jerks In My Career
None

P.S. As I proofread this book, I know one thing for sure: I've inadvertently left out some names I should have included and for purposes of time and space have eliminated some stories I was anxious to use—enough for at least one more book. The Good Lord and Father Time willing, it'll be along some day soon.

Stand by.

Jack Brickhouse